110668284

Opening Minds: A Journey of Extraordinary Encounters, Crop Circles, and Resonance.

By Simeon Hein, Ph.D.

Mount Baldy Press, Inc., Boulder, Colorado
A Division of the Institute for Resonance.

Opening Minds: A Journey of Extraordinary Encounters, Crop Circles, and Resonance

Mount Baldy Press
P.O. Box 469
Boulder, CO 80306-0469
To order, call 1-800-247-6553
orders@mountbaldy.com
www.MountBaldy.com

Covers and Illustrations © 2002 by Ira Liss
Cover Photo: Milkhill "Galaxy Formation" © 2001 by
Peter R. Sorensen

Edited by Jennifer Quinn

First Edition: June, 2002
Second Edition: July, 2002
Third Edition, First Printing: August, 2002
Printed in the United States of America

Publisher's Cataloging-in-Publication

Hein, Simeon.
Opening Minds : a journey of extraordinary encounters, crop circles, and resonance / by Simeon Hein.
p. cm.
Includes bibliographic references and index.
LCCN 2002100198
ISBN 0-9715863-0-6

1. Parapsychology and science. 2. Remote viewing (Parapsychology) 3. Crop Circles. 4. Life on other planets I. Title

BF1045.S33H45 2002   133
                    QBI02-701117

Table of Contents

v

Figures

Acknowledgments

It is often said that truth is stranger than fiction, and this book may prove that point. However, it is a strangeness that is witnessed by many people. No one alone could have experienced all that is contained in the following story. Group consciousness, while experienced individually, is generated from a collective energy that transcends any one of us. Each individual adds a unique angle on the infinite mystery that surrounds us all.

Thanks to Ron Russell and Peter Sorensen for their wonderful crop formation photos and research; Matthew Williams and the Circle Makers for their dedication and amazing designs; Dr. Courtney Brown for getting me involved in viewing, and Lyn Buchanan for his patient and precise viewing instruction; Lorraine Moller for her resonant talents and inspirational support to write this book in the first place; Ira Liss, in addition to creating excellent graphics, provided motivational support that helped make the book a much bigger and more encompassing project than anything I had imagined. Jennifer Quinn was invaluable as my copy editor; Robin Williams helped the book to look great with some nifty fonts and formatting suggestions.

Gratitude also goes to the following people: Colin Andrews, Bob and Teri Brown, Prudence Calabrese, Jane Hawthorne, Maggie Caffrey, Dan Hoffacker, Teri Horton, Dan Iaria, Frances Lewis, Denise Lynch, Masao Maki, Minori Murata, Joleen Van Peursem, Robert Raith, Dr. Jonathan Reed, Don Miguel Ruiz, Dale Stephens, Deborah Stewart, Busty Taylor, Linda Territo, Steve Tsutsumi and many others for their continued support and willingness to dive into the mystery. Thanks also goes to everyone who has participated in some way in the Mount Baldy Institute in Boulder, CO. Experiences there have changed me forever.

Foreword

"What's the frequency, Kenneth?"

These were the only words that CBS Anchorman Dan Rather could recall from an unnerving experience in New York some years ago. Rather was accosted by two men on the street. He believed the men to be muggers, although there was no attempt to take his money—only the strange question, "What's the frequency, Kenneth?"

Today, an increasing number of people are asking, "What's the frequency?"

In a time of increasing dependence on materialism and technological devices, more and more people, including a good number of scientists, are coming to realize that the universe is connected in non-material ways.

Increasingly, the electromagnetic properties of the universe are being mentioned in studies over a wide range of disciplines, from physics to medicine.

The work of Dr. Raymond Royal Rife in the last century is paving the way toward understanding physical cures through the use of bio-electric energy. The "music of the spheres" is being understood in relation to sonic frequencies. Einstein's Unified Field Theory years ago advanced the concept that the entire universe is bound by an all encompassing vibrant energy field.

This concept, of course, may provide the explanation for the psychic phenomenon known as "remote viewing," a banal term

ix

devised by the U. S. military to obscure its intense interest in this psychic technology. During the 1970s and '80s, remote viewing was the object of one of the most intense, secret, scientific studies in recent times.

Remote viewing, or resonant viewing (RV), the make-up of the universe, and the fascinating crop circle phenomenon are the focal points of this book by Dr. Simeon Hein.

Beginning as an open-minded social scientist, Dr. Hein has undergone the same transformation from a narrowly-focused student of material reality to a truly aware member of the universal community, as did the members of the U. S. Government's GRILL FLAME and STAR GATE remote viewing units.

In *Opening Minds: A Journey of Extraordinary Encounters, Crop Circles, and Resonance*, Dr. Hein takes the reader on a thought-expanding tour of some of the latest scientific literature and studies which clearly demonstrate that individual human existence goes far beyond our daily workspace, social settings, and favorite sports or TV sitcoms.

Before taking a look at the intriguing but little publicized phenomenon of crop circles and remote viewing, readers are invited to take a look at themselves and our society.

It is a troubling view. As noted by comedian and social commentator George Carlin, we buy more, but enjoy less; have more conveniences, but less time; more experts, but more problems; more medicines, but less wellness; we conquered the atom, but not our prejudices; we learned to rush, but not to wait; we've learned to make a living, but not a life; we upgrade computers to hold more information, but we communicate less.

Dr. Hein sees that one way out of this cultural and societal morass may be through "resonant viewing," a version of remote viewing practiced at the Mount Baldy Institute for Resonant Viewing in Boulder, Colorado.

Through both descriptions and illustrations, Hein demonstrates both the validity and the power of the RV experience and how it might be applied to our understanding of our world.

Since the news of remote viewing first reached the public in 1995, various factions within and without the government have tried to decry its effectiveness. Yet, according to many different sources, RV is still being practiced deep within secret government units.

Why would government officials disparage a technology that they themselves are using? Simple. Knowledge is indeed power and they are determined to keep this power to themselves.

Consider what might happen if statements made on a national television address by the President were immediately called into question by various qualified remote viewers throughout the nation and the world? What if they publicly announced the real issues and motives behind his words? Centralized power and control could quickly be lost should the corporate mass media lend any credibility whatsoever to this purely human technology.

This is the power of remote viewing. The strenuous scientific studies at Stanford Research Institute proved that this power resides in each and every one of us, merely awaiting the proper training and discipline to be effectively utilized.

We are all material beings energized by the vibrant frequencies of the universe. We are a powerful and creative species crippled only by ourselves, our conditioning, and our environment. It is time to regain our rightful place as truly free and creative members of the universal community.

The empowering information in this book, accompanied by an openness to new thoughts and technologies, could change lives. After all, your mind is like a parachute . . . it works much better when it's open.

Jim Marrs
Author of *Alien Agenda*, *Crossfire*, and *Psi Spies*
Texas, USA, December, 2001

xi

Preface

As a graduate student in sociology during the early 1990s, I learned how to study the world from a systematic and scientific point of view. Like many other social scientists, I was fairly confident that I knew how the world could be studied and how to make sense of it. In graduate school, I was introduced to ideas about linear causation, cause and effect, and statistics. These tools were supposed to help me understand the world in a rational, methodological way. By the time I left graduate school, I thought those tools were all I needed.

However, I was soon to encounter extraordinary phenomena that defied conventional explanation. These phenomena were not linear nor consistently observable, and yet they appeared often enough to convince me they were real. They didn't fit the pattern or definitions of what I had been taught were the boundaries of reality. Yet their existence was undeniable. I was to learn that the principles underlying this non-ordinary reality rested on an entirely different theoretical basis than I was familiar with.

Shortly after to moving to Boulder, Colorado in 1996, I was introduced to remote viewing: the ability of a person to perceive, acquire, and describe non-local information. I wasn't against the idea of remote viewing—I just didn't believe I could do it myself. Subsequent events were to prove me wrong and turn my whole world upside down. The following is an account of my personal journey into the world of the unknown,—a place of spirit spaces where the material world is left behind; a place where a hidden intelligence mysteriously orchestrates reality from behind the scenes. I can't say that I understand exactly what these events are all about; but they happened and I describe them here to the best of my ability.

Simeon Hein, Ph.D.

Introduction

WE LIVE IN A WORLD that is increasingly dependent upon complex technology. During the last century we have experienced a flood of new types of information technologies including cellular phones, fax machines, and satellite communications. Interplanetary exploration is becoming increasingly common, and private astronauts are readying themselves for space adventures. Everywhere you look, computers and other electronic gadgets are finding new roles in activities where they were previously absent. We constantly hear the media talk about broadband connectivity, Internet access, and faster ways to move information around the planet. No other civilization on our planet (that we know of) has ever experienced such rapid technological change.

Yet despite the plethora of technological advances that propel our society, we often feel increasingly disconnected, rushed, and frustrated in our lives. We experience a gnawing sense of anxiety and feel we can never get enough accomplished during each day. While technology has increased the amount of external information available to us, it has also increased the amount of work expected of us. In some respects, we have become more impoverished internally. We feel we have less time now than ever before. Our days often seem preoccupied with the trivia of computer malfunctions, software glitches, and TV channel surfing. In the midst of our fascination and preoccupation with electronic technology, we seem to have become out of tune with the natural technologies built into all of us. Compared to our inherent human abilities, the external technology we are using is limited and brittle, with little room for flexibility or evolution. In many situations, our machines seem to make things simultaneously over-complicated and cumbersome. Like the latest computer components, they are full of potential—and yet unreliable, non-emotional and inaccessible to our ordinary understanding.

Part of the reason for this frustration is that we are still clinging to an outworn belief system that was put into place several hundred years ago during the Scientific Revolution of Isaac Newton, Réne Descartes, and others. In this world-view, the universe is seen as a big, uniform machine, its gears running according to pre-established rules independent of its environment; life is a result of physical and mechanical laws where organisms are simply the sum of the total activity of their individual pieces. The universe, in essence, can be reduced to a finite set of building blocks operating according to a finite set of laws. From this perspective, once we know all the parts and the laws governing their interaction we should (in theory) be able to explain everything that happens around us. We can fight diseases with new medicines, send a man to the moon, and get better weather predictions.

Despite the success of the Newtonian-Cartesian paradigm and the material wealth it has helped to produce, this is a limited view which is inapplicable to the universe below the atomic scale. Discoveries in quantum physics shortly after the turn of the nineteenth century were able to show this perspective to be fundamentally limited and in many ways incorrect. Time and space are not quantities independent of the objects they contain. Things that appear solid are actually bundles or waves of energy in mostly empty space. The act of observation affects what is being observed. And consciousness is not the epiphenomenon of matter. In fact, quantum physics tells us just the opposite: It states we are in a living universe where consciousness and thought create matter. This matter is the condensation of energy and information in a vast field that exists outside of time and space. From this point of view, the universe is not a machine at all nor a collection of rocks and hot gasses, but rather a huge, conscious entity composed of an infinitely complex web of interactions between particles, things, and organisms.

Notwithstanding all the evidence that supports the quantum view and all of its resulting implications, our society is still experiencing a form of cultural lag whereby our belief systems are oriented to the scientific views of the last century. The fundamental ideas that we hold true are, in many respects, geared to an outmoded paradigm. While we know that the Earth is a living system and that our individual actions affect life on every level, many of us still live our lives as if we were in a vacuum and fail to see ourselves as an integral part of our environment. The vast types of environmental and social problems that afflict our world will attest to our adherence of anachronistic belief systems. We have become prisoners of our own limited, collective ideas that are based on mechanistic assumptions we know to be false. As a result, we suffer higher levels of collective stress, strain, and scarcity than are necessary.

In contrast to mechanistic systems and monoculture- producing machines, nature operates on the basis of an inherent intelligence that is spontaneous, coherent, and still very precise. Living organisms are not like machines at all, as they are capable of self-repair, evolution, and adaptability. The principles that guide organisms may originate in the hidden quantum field of intelligence, and thus the network that connects living things with one another is infinitely more "broadband" and responsive than mechanically constructed systems will ever be.

To take just one example of how quantum physics differs from the Newtonian paradigm, consider the idea of non-locality. According to the Newtonian perspective, for one object to affect another, it must affect all other intervening space between the two objects. So for two objects to interact, they have to be physically connected in some way, like gears in a car or billiard balls in a game of pool.

Yet for subatomic particles, this is not true at all. A particle can move from one space to another without moving in the intervening space between the two positions. Particles can also be correlated to other particles no matter how far apart they are in physical space. This principle of non-locality, known as Bell's Theorem, is backed by numerous experiments and is one of the fundamental ideas of the quantum view (Goswami, *The Self-Aware Universe* 1993). Bell showed that two particles, once correlated, would always remain correlated no matter how far apart they were from one another. This is known as "quantum entanglement." The implications of just this one idea alone are momentous because it implies that space is not a barrier to the flow of information as it is in the Newtonian view. This view also suggests that living things are characterized by fields of internal, self-organized processes—innate communications abilities that are not part of external, mechanistic, and intentionally constructed systems.

Collectively, however, we continue to think in a mechanistic way, as if there were only one optimal solution to every problem. We prefer rigid, hierarchically-ordered control systems to flexible ones; quick-fix solutions over slower, evolutionary alternatives. Favoring homogeneity over diversity, we continue to push our planet to ever-greater levels of tension and disintegration. Rather than let natural solutions emerge from our own inner intelligence and nature's infinite adaptability, we still look to old ways of thinking and the traditional political and cultural institutions associated with them. Many of these institutions are based on outmoded belief systems.

For example, we still look to so-called experts for answers rather than to our own inner wisdom. Recent statistics discussed by the media in late 1999 suggested that up to 100,000 people are killed annually in hospitals from improperly applied medical treatments, a number that exceeds deaths due to auto accidents. Our trust in formal systems and experts often has negative consequences. Instead, our perception should be redirected within ourselves to provide the answers.

Intrinsic to the spread of the quantum paradigm is a shift in focus from external systems to internal systems. This shift has widespread ramifications in how we live and think about ourselves and our world. To deal with contemporary challenges we should apply our best understanding of how nature works and question long-held assumptions. Quantum physics suggests that the universe is considerably more malleable, adaptable, and aware than previous scientific world-views acknowledged. Furthermore, the quantum view puts us in the commander's seat of the universe because it recognizes that our thought processes steer the ship we call "physical reality"—rather than the other way around.

The Physics of Resonance

Resonant viewing, more traditionally known as "remote viewing," represents one practical application of quantum processes: those interactions that are based on the internal dynamics of living systems. Resonant technologies represent a leap forward in the integration of our mind, body, and spirit. Already incorporated in modern technology, principles of quantum energy and resonance are the foundation of a plethora of devices that include communication systems and new modes of energy-matter transformation. More importantly, any person with little in the way of external equipment can access these principles. Using simple protocols, resonant viewing allows a person to act like a tuning fork, selectively picking up distant information regarding specific people, places, and events. Powerful, yet simple in practice, RV directly accesses our quantum minds giving us the ability to transcend space and time in order to perceive all types of non-local information. If we collectively tap into this intelligence, we are no longer enslaved to closed, externally manufactured systems. In the RV process, a person can have direct contact with different types of energy and information that are inaccessible to mechanistic processes and systems that operate from a reductionist point of view. When individuals realize they have the inherent ability to create their own solutions, the source of our authority shifts from external mechanisms to our innate intelligence. With the application of these quantum principles, humans can achieve new levels of coherency, spontaneity, and precision. By bringing these principles into our daily lives, we can think and behave in a more integrated way and so provide progressive thinking to global challenges. Once we re-evaluate our assumptions and beliefs about reality in light of these new paradigms, it is possible for nature and culture to harmoniously evolve together.

Quantum Fields

Parallel to the development of resonant viewing in recent years, there has been an increasing proliferation of crop formations around the world. Crop formations are geometric patterns, flattened and swirled, that have been appearing in grain crops since recorded history began. The earliest accounts have gone back to the Bible. These formations have taken place in many countries, especially in the last one hundred years, with increasing proliferation in the last two decades. Since the 1980s, over ten thousand of these formations have appeared around the globe. The evidence surrounding these events suggests that this phenomenon is more complex than meets the eye with differing levels of human, paranormal, and psychic interactions. Well-documented evidence of battery and camera failures, balls of light, UFOs, and precognitive experiences surrounding the crop formations suggests that they operate in an out-of-the-ordinary manner. Participants in the form of human circle-makers (circle-facilitators as I call them)and researchers continue to experience events that could only be ascribed to unknown physical principles. The circles bring forth new forms of vibration and frequency that create novel resonant interactions which are unexplainable with our current paradigm.

And paralleling both the increasing public awareness of the existence of RV and crop circles has been a steady and concentrated flow of information about UFOs and extraterrestrials. Our mental programming is gradually shifting to the acceptance of the reality of extraterrestrial life on our own planet Earth. Information has come forth from a combination of sources, such as the late Colonel Philip Corso, Dr. Steven Greer, and other experts including the attorney Daniel Sheehan, as well as Dr. Roger Leir, who has surgically removed foreign implants from people's bodies. The weight of the evidence is beginning to show that we are not alone in the universe and that off-planet visitors are here with us now. It suggests that our nation and world are being prepared for eventual participation in interstellar forms of contact and communication—an experience that will completely and irrevocably change the way we live and think about ourselves and the cosmos forever.

It appears that our current technological revolution is being paralleled by a revolution in our consciousness as we begin to realize the interconnectedness of our minds, bodies, and the environments we live in. This is not necessarily an esoteric or mystical experience, but a practical way to adapt and evolve out of the zero-sum box into a win-win situation on a universal scale. Just as technology is on a relentless path to connecting us externally, our ability to manage and program our internal, mental software is also growing exponentially. As we become more globally integrated, our awareness of our inner universe is expanding. With the newfound ability to experiment with our awareness also comes a new sense of responsibility and accountability. Perhaps we have finally arrived at an age where we can consciously transform our planet into a healthier and more balanced place to live.

Holographic Potentials

Holograms are interference patterns that are embedded in a two-dimensional film surface. To the naked eye a hologram looks like a sheet of blurry concentric rings; however, when a laser is sent through the image it produces a coherent 3-dimensional shape projected into space. These are often seen in toyshops, Disneyland, and on credit cards. A hologram has the ability to trick our eye into believing a fully 3-dimensional object is in front of us. It has been suggested by researchers like Karl Pribram (neuroscientist) and David Bohm (physicist), that holographic principles are at work in our bodies and throughout the world (Talbott, 1992). Their basic idea is that every bit of space contains the whole universe and our experience in the universe derives from this reality.

In a holographic universe any point is accessible from any other point. We all have the ability to change the "channels" we are perceiving, as all possibilities are equidistant to us. The idea of holography also suggests that everything exists in context. In contrast to the disassociated information that our technology tends to feed us, the natural way of the universe is that everything down to the finest details are completely embedded in a context. This also lends support to the idea of non-locality, as the information in a hologram is located in the whole pattern, not in a specific place in the film. Paying attention to this pattern is what allows a person to move from one resonant frequency or reality to the next.

Organization of the Book

This book is organized as follows: Chapter 1, "The Resonant Challenge," investigates some of the impacts of the mechanistic world-view on our lives and how these ideas have become antiquated. Recently, the advent of the quantum perspective in our century has seriously undermined some of the traditional, classical beliefs we hold about the nature of reality. The world and universe are not so much machines as they are self-aware fields of energy and information. The principles of "quantum entanglement" suggest that particles, even though separated by miles of distance, still behave like one pair simultaneously reacting to the each other. Separation by space does not necessarily create energetic separation. Reductionism, so common to modern science, is too inadequate to deal with the complexities and paradoxes of the quantum perspective. The rise in popularity of fractal geometry (the mathematics of natural shapes) illustrates the inherent limits of reductionism, as fractals have an infinite degree of detail. Just like nature, fractals can be magnified to see more of the structure of something like our lungs or cardiovascular system with its tens of thousands of miles of veins and arteries. Fractal structures tend to repeatedly branch out for a long distance and, unlike our technological systems, they do not resolve into lines. This creates vast avenues for the communication that penetrate many different levels. Chaotic interactions arise out of these nonlinear interactions. Similarly, quantum systems are integrated in a way that makes the spontaneous exchange of information possible, an idea inconceivable to the classical point of view of physics.

Chapters 2 and 3 are academically oriented investigations of time, the development of information technology, and how we collectively got to be where we are today. Chapter 2, "Technology and Time Control," examines the nature of time and the ways in which technology has changed our use of time. Once part of a natural, seamless flow, time is now controlled by artificial, discrete machine processes designed to maximize efficiency at the cost of our holistic integration in our environments. Our separation from nature starts with the clock.

Chapter 3, "The Age of Missing Information," explores the way in which our modern technology destroys information. Increased speed and flow of digital information serves to fragment our attention rather than make us more informed. Our mass media has become increasingly mentally impoverished, and the instant forms of communication available to us do not enhance our understanding of our world as much as they flood our attention with unrelated facts and symbols. Technology is not a substitute for the holistic quality of self-organized, spontaneously developing systems. If you are not interested in this type of historical discussion, feel free to skip to Chapter 4.

Chapter 4, "Resonant Viewing" outlines the basics of resonant viewing and how I came to be involved in this area of research. I describe the different aspects of a viewing session and the role of the subconscious mind in the process. I also discuss how the subconscious mind is connected to the universal matrix of information. I'll introduce the idea of the body as a signal processor and how viewing bypasses the conscious mind, allowing a person's perceptual doorways to open up. Specifically, I discuss the role of the chaos theory in resonant viewing and how chaotic brain states allow a person access to a wider range of etheric frequencies. I'll also describe some of the more "out-of-ordinary" experiences that myself and other people have occasionally encountered after immersing ourselves in RV. I also explain why I believe that "resonant viewing" is a more accurate name for the process than "remote viewing."

Chapter 5, "Discovering the Alien Within" discusses my remote viewing experiences at the Farsight Institute of Atlanta, Georgia, and how I was introduced to the reality of extraterrestrials through actual viewing sessions. The chapter will illustrate the amazing experiences of my colleagues with what appear to be off-planet entities.

Chapter 6, "Liquid Landscapes," discusses the mystery of crop circles and how I came to the subject. I discuss some of the history of the phenomena and my own research into the field. I mention some of the strange experiences that many people and myself have experienced in association with crop formations and how this relates to resonant viewing. Recently we have learned that, in some parts of the world, people are directly involved in the phenomenon, and I offer some explanation of why human-facilitated formations may create anomalous activity such as balls of light, UFOs, and electronic machine failure. I'll also suggest some ideas as to how human-made formations are introducing us to a new dimension of the unknown.

Chapter 7, "Interfacing with the Unknown" introduces the idea of subtle energies and how crop formations and resonant viewing are related to these "ultra-weak" energies. There is an increasing amount of information about this subject and it promises to bring us to a whole new understanding of our universe and ourselves. Subtle energies, like quantum mechanics, defy the principles of classical physics, yet we know they are real. Integrating this knowledge into our lives promises to change how we live completely. If we are to become full-fledged members of the galactic community, we must first evolve and grow to meet our own "inner aliens." In doing so, we will shift our own personal and collective frequencies and in the process open up our perception to a larger universe.

Part I. Nature, Mechanization, and Resonance

1. Diving Into the Unknown:
The Resonant Challenge

IN EDWIN ABBOTT'S CLASSIC book, *Flatland*, written in 1884, the inhabitants of a two-dimensional land live in a world of limited space and belief systems. Occupying the area on a flat surface, the different shapes that live in Flatland believe that only flat shapes are real and that solid three-dimensional shapes are folk tales and superstition. They also believe that specific characteristics of one's shape determine their worth. Social status in Flatland is based on one's number of sides and geometrical coherency. When a three-dimensional object, a sphere from Spaceland appears to a Flatlander one day, the latter believes it to be from the realm of the supernatural. However, he is taken on a trip to Spaceland by the sphere and becomes convinced of the reality of higher dimensions. When he returns to Flatland and tells of his travels, he is arrested and imprisoned. His new-found belief system is a threat to the flat world's social system, and he is therefore locked up indefinitely.

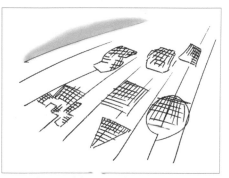

In Edwin Abbott's classic, Flatland, an inhabitant of a two-dimensional land discovers a 3D world.

A square from Flatland discovers a sphere from Spaceland.

In our own time, the recent movie *Pleasantville* made a similar point. Here the inhabitants in the town of Pleasantville live in a black and white world, their knowledge of the cosmos goes no further than the boundaries of their town. They are emotionally superficial and unchallenged, until some of them begin to experience genuine emotions, and are able to see in color. Gradually their attitudes spread to the rest of the town, and everyone begins to experience this three-dimensional emotional life. In the end, they have moved from complacency, through chaos, into a new social and cultural order.

Like the inhabitants of Flatland and Pleasantville, we too have been brought up in a world of limited beliefs that we often take for granted. While events occasionally occur that jar our sense of reality, we are often too eager to rationalize these experiences away and then easily forget about them. We often prefer comfort to the challenge of personal and social growth. However, just like the denizens of flat or black-and-white worlds, a new reality is fast approaching our town. This reality has been steadily building and fortifying its solidity over the past century and is now on the brink of engulfing all previous paradigms in its wake. As this new paradigm approaches, we see signs on the edges

The square becomes multidimensional.

of our perceptual horizon that reality is changing. The new paradigm is one based on the idea of multidimensional resonance.

The idea of resonance in and of itself is not hard to understand. For example, think of two tuning forks. Anyone who has used these to tune a musical instrument knows that if two tuning forks are tuned to the same pitch, when one is struck they both will vibrate. They resonant together because they are tuned to the same frequency. Experiments in quantum mechanics have shown that two sub-atomic particles, once they have interacted, will remain correlated even if they are separated by a billion miles. This suggests that even when particles are physically separated, they still occupy the same vibrational space. In some ways, they are not separated at all because they share a common frequency. Thus, the principle of resonance can operate at the quantum level and also at the level of physical reality.

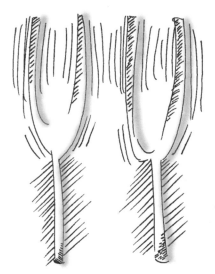

Tuning forks resonate together when tuned to the same frequency. Living beings also resonate to subtle frequencies.

Much has been written about this subtle type of energy interaction. Researchers have described these subtle energies as "ultra-weak" forces because they are difficult to measure. Others have labeled these energies as "non-Hertzian" because they defy electromagnetic principles of space and time. Whatever we call this type of energy interaction, it is clear that quantum resonance in particular undermines the whole basis of mechanistic and reductionist thought systems. It is a shared frequency rather than a force that is at the center of our experience. Intrinsic to the idea of frequency is the notion of non-locality or "spooky action at a distance" (as Albert Einstein referred to it).

Subtle energies are not just descriptive of very small-scale phenomena. They are relevant to all levels of reality because the physical make-up of the universe is a collective of quantum energies: they appear solid under some circumstances and as waves under others. Therefore, physical matter is ultimately made up of a matrix of blips of energy and light. In this way, resonance and frequency permeate all levels of reality.

The Quantum Perspective

The worldview we have collectively inherited from the previous century is one of mechanism and reductionism. The mechanistic perspective, consistent with the worldviews of Descartes and Newton, sees the universe as a giant machine composed of gears and parts. This machine works according to linear principles of causation. Everything that happens in this machine is observable and explainable in simple, empirical terms. Consistent with this belief system, is that of reductionism whereby the operation of the whole machine can be reduced to the

Newtonian physics sees the universe as a system of direct cause and effect.

sum of the parts. These parts are observable, discrete units that determine the properties of the whole machine. The viewpoint also contains a linear idea of time and space where things happen in a sequential, causal order.

The limitations of this perspective are evident when considered in light of the quantum perspective. According to quantum physics, the world beyond the level of atoms is not a solid mass but rather a fluctuating field of energy. The world's solid appearance is in some senses an illusion generated by our sensory organs. At the very smallest states of matter, what appears solid, is not. Also, the state of the quantum fields is affected by who is observing them so they can take the form of a wave or a particle depending on the situation. This implies that the way we see the world is a product of how we think about it: the form is not intrinsically built into external reality; rather, our belief structure is the ultimate arbiter of reality.

There is also the related notion of "quantum entanglement." This is the idea that particles, once they interact, always interact. Even separated by a billion miles, they still behave like a pair and can affect each other at a distance.

Fractal Flatteners vs. Fractal Fatteners

Just like Flatland, we live in a world that is increasingly made of square and flattened shapes—the stuff of traditional Euclidian geometry. These shapes are consistent with a rationalized economy designed for efficiency, control and speed. Things are designed to get done in the quickest amount of time possible, machines keep running, and our economy continues to buzz along. This perspective has produced untold amounts of material wealth and abundance. Yet nature works with a different logic, the logic of fractal geometry—irregular, detailed, grainy, yet ordered shapes.

Fractals were first discovered by mathematicians at the turn of the last century, but shunned because of their geometrical uncertainty. Since fractals can be magnified indefinitely, they have no resolution point, as does a simple line. There is an infinite amount of detail in a fractal shape, the word "fractal" coming from the word "fractured."

In modern times, Benoit Mandelbrot, a mathematician at IBM, studied the problem of telephone line noise in the 1970's. He found that the shape of the noise was roughly the same at any scale you looked at it. This is called "self-similarity." Whether the scale was one hour or one minute the noise spikes had the same appearance and frequency. Mandelbrot compared these phenomena to the coastline of England: The distance between two points depends on the size of your ruler. A ruler 1-foot long would measure the coastline differently from a ruler 1-inch long, as the shorter ruler could detect smaller spaces than the larger ruler. A really tiny ruler would be able to measure even smaller spaces. Thus, linear measurements of fractal systems are mere approximations and not absolute.

Equally important was Mandelbrot's identification of a class of objects that exist between standard dimensions. That is, the coastline of England is more than a 1-dimensional line and less than a 2-dimensional plane: its dimension is between 1 and 2. Similarly, a cloud takes up more space than a 2-dimensional plane but less than a 3-dimensional cube: if you magnify a cloud you would find that in-between the water droplets is empty space, and therefore the cloud is not solid. Therefore its fractal dimension is somewhere between 2 and 3. If you were to estimate it accurately, a cloud's fractal dimension is around 2.2 or 2.3.

"Self-similarity" is a phenomenon where the shape of a pattern, noise, or process is the same at any scale of observation.

Figure 1 is a computer-generated fractal that resembles a tree. Notice the self-similarity of the branches and increasing amount of detail, as you look closer and closer at the picture. This shows that nature often works along principles of fractal mathematics.

Fractal principles can also be used to create artwork of great beauty. Figure 2 was created by video-grapher Peter Sorensen using the computer program *Bryce*. This picture was created on a computer using fractals and the idea of self-similarity. Thus the picture, even though created electronically, retains the natural feeling that is characteristic of real objects and landscapes. The picture is multidimensional rather than linear.

These examples illustrate the idea of fractal dimension: a non-integer whole number that measures a complex system with nooks, crannies, and lots of detail. Real-world objects tend to be approximated by fractal rather than integer dimensions. Fractal structures have lots of branches, like trees. The more closely you look, the more detail you see. The object never resolves to a line. The dynamics of these types of systems is that they tend to behave chaotically rather than linearly. They work in unpredictable ways. Our heart and brain-wave patterns, for example, while showing a great deal of coherency over a long period of time, tend to fluctuate from moment to moment. While stable heart and brain patterns used to be considered indicators of a healthy body, new research suggests that chaotic patterns are healthier than stable patterns (Goldberger and West, 1987; Goldberger, Rigney, and West, 1990).

Music is a good example of a chaotic system. When listening to music one cannot always predict exactly what note will follow the next. And each note only makes sense in the context of the whole piece; each note by itself would be meaningless. Music is not always predictable and yet, at the same time, not always random.

Studies of music from all over the world show that all cultures create music that has a similar distribution of notes. There always tends to be more variation in treble note patterns than in bass note patterns. This suggests that music follows hidden chaotic rules producing order and variability in an intelligent—yet nonlinear—way.

Figure 1: A Fractal Tree

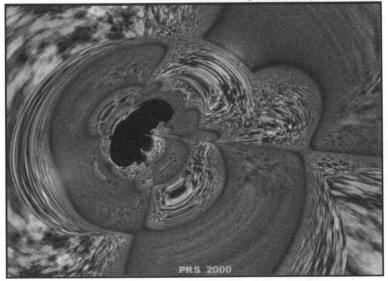

Figure 2: Bryce Drawing

One of the reasons nature uses fractal geometry in biological systems is because fractal structures maximize the amount of information or energy flow within a system with a finite amount of space. Our bodies, for example, exist within a finite physical space. To provide a maximum surface area for blood vessels in our cardiovascular system, our arteries continually branch out into smaller and smaller tubes. This allows as much oxygen flow within our bodies as possible. The fractal structure of our lungs and cardiovascular system allows for the greatest exchange of oxygen and waste gasses between the lungs, blood, and body cells. The branching structure of our veins, arteries, and capillaries extends for tens of thousands of miles throughout our body thanks to their fractal, branching structure. Similarly, our nervous systems have a fractal distribution starting from the central main nerves and ending up smaller. Branching fractal structures increase surface contact with a living system and in doing so increases the flow of chemicals and information throughout the organism. Fractal processes pack as much material as possible into limited spaces.

A tree gathers as much sunlight as possible with its leaves. The fractal structures of the branches serve to maximize the amount of tree surface that is exposed to the sun. If the tree were composed of flat surfaces, it would not get as much light. Thus, jagged complicated surfaces rather than smooth ones maximize flow-through.

The fractal shape of nature is built around a type of time other than a linear system—"deep" time. This time is not connected from moment to moment in a linear way, but at many different levels and in many ways. Fractal time is chaotic yet ordered, intuitive, spontaneous, integrated and intelligent. This allows organisms the maximum number of evolutionary possibilities.

In contrast, many of our technologically-based systems tend to be based in Euclidean geometry using shapes such as circles or squares. The logic is one of efficiency rather than effectiveness, so the shapes tend to be sleek or very boxy. These systems are more linear than self-similar. Machine-time is external, repetitive and mechanistic; it creates a world dominated by clocks and time-keeping devices. However, fractal-based systems and organisms are self-regulating and self-organized.

In addition to the physical function of fractal shapes, it is possible that fractals serve as etheric antennae with their ever- branching limbs. In a sense, fractals are like a form of natural technology that humans are just beginning to use. One of the practical applications of fractals has been in compressing data sets to fit into smaller spaces. With specific algorithms, a computer can squeeze a given amount of data into a smaller space, easing capacities of satellites or computer image processing programs. With a picture, for example, the pixels can be sampled and then discarded, reducing the size of the file. Then using the fractal algorithm and the compressed data set, the picture can be accurately reproduced at another time, saving storage space or bandwidth.

Studies of music from all over the world show a similar fractal distribution of notes. There tends to be more variation in treble notes than in bass note patterns.

By analogy, our bodies may work in a similar way, picking up faint signals here or there in the quantum field and then decompressing the information until we can fully perceive and interpret it. In a resonant viewing session, the viewer can sometimes fully describe the visuals or concepts of an object or person just from decoding their ideograms. These ideograms function as holographic fractal signatures that contain a wealth of information in their shape. Thus, the missing information in our technological world may be compensated by the innate intelligence of nature and our physical bodies. Our biology may be designed to juncture with etheric types of information. Future technology could be designed to work with this mind/body interface.

The Butterfly Effect

One of the interesting implications of fractal research is that objects with fractal shapes tend to have chaotic dynamics. Edward Lorenz at MIT (Massachusetts Institute of Technology) first observed this in the 1960s. Lorenz was studying the predictability of weather systems. He originally thought that with the proper computer program it would be possible to perfectly predict the weather. He soon found out that even the slightest change in the initial conditions of the weather system could completely change the weather a few days hence. He labeled this phenomenon as the "Butterfly Effect." In essence, the weather is so sensitive that under the right conditions, a butterfly flapping its wings over the Amazon rainforest could affect the weather in Japan.

The Butterfly Effect implies that many systems are inherently unpredictable. They are so sensitive to small and subtle changes that there is no computer powerful enough (nor will there ever be) to calculate all the conditions of the variables that affect the system. Living organisms in particular are part of that mold of things that often cannot be predicted. Similarly, the spontaneous fluctuations in our minds and bodies defy the ability of anything to tell us exactly what they will be doing in the future. Chaos theory is another challenge to the mechanistic, classical paradigm because it says that self-generated processes from within a system generate change; change is not generated merely by measurable forces from without.

The Conscious Mind as Editor

The ancient Polynesians were said to be able to navigate the entire Pacific Ocean simply by their knowledge of bird flight patterns, ocean currents, and the positions of the stars. Or consider the knowledge that went into the hand-made construction of building materials, musical instruments, or artwork. Today this information is often the sole prerogative of corporations that protect their ideas with patents and armies of lawyers. In the past, information was passed down from generation to generation. This was information that absorbs all our senses and awareness. This type of information has a much broader meaning than the contents of our home-page that loads when we connect our web browser to the Internet. Because in a large sense, what we call "information" today is simply data and nothing more. And data by itself without meaningful interpretation is useless.

Another important point about information is the relatively limited amount that we consciously perceive from the outside world. Our neurophysiology acts as a strong filtering mechanism. Recent research indicates that we are conscious of less than one-tenth of one percent of the information that comes into our brains every second; that's 16 bits out of 40 million bits (Norretranders, pp. 126-8, 1997). In other words, our consciousness acts like a funnel straining out the vast bulk of the information that the mind deems is unneeded. Consciousness, it seems, spends most of its energy throwing out what it considers to be frivolous information, unnecessary to our immediate survival or short-term needs. Our belief systems determine what gets retained and what does not. In a real sense, what we perceive is a sensory representation of our belief systems, not physical reality.

Our hidden intelligence, on the other hand, seems to work more effectively through our subconscious mind as opposed to our conscious mind. Because it is subconscious, this part of our awareness works best if we don't interfere with it. The subconscious has the responsibility to process and integrate information from outside ourselves. We take in this information all the time but the vast majority of the information is below the limen, the threshold of our awareness. Thus, as the motivational counselor Anthony Robbins suggests, we truly are "deletion creatures." Much of the information is still there, it is just buried in our subconscious.

copyright Ira Liss

Our conscious mind is aware of less than one-tenth of one percent of the information that comes into our senses: that's 16 bits out of 10 millions per second! Our consciousness acts like a funnel straining out the vast bulk of information our senses receive.

Dreamtime

In a very real sense, we suffer today from a lack of natural experiences and interactions due to the overwhelming presence of machines and processed environments in our world. Our mind's intrinsic tendency to narrow our internal information highway reduces our experience even further. The net result is that we do not have a full spectrum of information resources available to us, like we once had. Just as we can purchase light bulbs that emit a full spectrum of light, we need to pay attention to the possibility that we may be missing a full spectrum of experiences in our day-to-day existence. The Aborigines of Australia have the idea of the "Dreamtime": a place outside of linear space-time where one interacts with one's energy body and that of the planet, free from physical and social constraints. Those of us in the West have no such equivalent of Dreamtime, and so our awareness and mental energies have no place to go for release. As a substitute we accept the mechanized dreaming of television with its routine and programmed displays of violence and silliness. However, the Dreamtime potential our own mind creates vastly exceeds anything that could ever be shown on television. The following passage from Robert Lawlor's book *Voices of the First Day* (1991) illustrates the sensitivity of indigenous people to very specific vibrational frequencies:

> In the Aboriginal world view, every meaningful activity, event, or life process that occurs at a particular place leaves behind a vibrational residue in the earth, as plants leave an image of themselves as seeds. The shape of the land - its mountains, rocks, riverbeds, and waterholes - and its unseen vibrations echo the events that brought that place into creation. Everything in the natural world is a symbolic footprint of the metaphysical beings whose actions created our world. As with a seed, the potency of an earthly location is wedded to the memory of its origin. The Aborigines called this potency the "Dreaming" of a place, and this Dreaming constitutes the sacredness of the earth. Only in extraordinary states of consciousness can one be aware of, or attuned to, the inner dreaming of the earth (p. 1).

Thus, as we pay more attention to our intuitive, hidden intelligence, we become aware of the native intelligence of the planet and the plethora of energy fields that exist here.

Synchronicity

As we experience more fractal time in our lives, we also tend to have more synchronicities happen to us. Synchronicity occurs when a seemingly unlikely event happens in an effortless, coordinated way, almost as if by magic. *Chronos* (time) becomes synthesized in seemingly unrelated events and occurrences. The quantum level of reality works in this effortless way because at a deeper level everything is connected and interrelated. Resonant viewing, by matching frequencies from seemingly distant events, people, and places creates a coordination at a quantum level that has repercussions at all levels of physical reality. Thus, the process of engaging and interacting with resonance increases the likelihood that synchronistic experiences will occur.

Synchronicity shows us there is a deeper level of reality operating around us all the time. Our conscious mind is oblivious to this level of reality, yet this type of apparently random experience shows that the universe has an underlying order that is orchestrated by an unseen intelligence. This underlying order can be activated by our own intent and thus seems to be a permanent feature of biophysical reality.

The amazing thing is not that synchronicity happens, but why it doesn't happen constantly at every moment. Or perhaps it happens so often that we don't notice it.

The Body as Signal Processor

For many of us, thinking of our body as an energy processor may conjure up images of daily jobs with their nine to five routines and regular paychecks. For hundreds of years we have been conditioned to coordinate our work life with the mechanical rhythms of clocks and calendars. But inside the field of the human body is another type of etheric machine that has infinitely more calculating power than any device created by modern technology. Our bodies are constantly processing trillions of interactions per second among hundreds of billions of cells. There is more going on in our bodies per second than we could ever possibly imagine and the vast majority of those interactions are on autopilot. We don't have to think about them because this hidden, yet essential, activity of our cells and organs is orchestrated by the innate intelligence of our body/mind. This innate intelligence works at the level of our cells and within our subconscious mind to coordinate not only our bodies but our interactions with the outside world.

Within each of us is this river of hidden intelligence. Beneath the noise and turbulence of our conscious minds lies a hidden realm of awareness that we may not even realize exists. The river of intelligence flows all the time to the changing seasons of our emotions, physiological conditions, and mental states. Most importantly, we can fish from this river anytime we want. The fish we catch from this river are the compilation of intuitions, hunches, and gut feelings—the raw particles of our intuition. The fish can be very healthy and nutritious, if we only learn to cook and eat them properly.

Kittens and Sea Captains

At the end of the sixteenth century, European sea captains set sail for different parts of the globe that were previously unknown and unexplored. One common experience reported by Columbus, Magellan, Cook, and Darwin was that the indigenous peoples they encountered in different parts of the world could not see their ships docked off shore. Not seeing the ships, the indigenous peoples could not imagine how the explorers arrived there. After some explaining by the captains, the natives would first see what appeared to them as a mountain on the water. Often the medicine man, accustomed to seeing outside the bounds of traditional culture, would be first to see the ships. Eventually people could see the ships after several hours or days.

The natives could not see something that did not fit into their conceptual scheme of reality, their mindset. Even though the light from the ships reached their eyes, their brains did not register the ships as real. Once it was explained to them what they could expect to see, they could perceive it. This confirms the idea that reality is a product of our belief system, rather than inherently objective phenomenon.

Studies done at Harvard Medical School with young kittens showed a similar effect. Kittens raised in rooms with only horizontal lines would end up bumping into vertical objects when taken to the outside world. Kittens raised in environments with only vertical lines could not see horizontal objects later on. This shows that our early upbringing and instilled belief system determine what aspects of reality we perceive. This reality system dictated by our culture becomes hardwired into our brains, remaining there unless we actively reprogram it.

Technology and the Fractal Flattening of our Perception

Like kittens and indigenous peoples, we have become conditioned to perceive only a slice of reality. Our perception has become narrowed to the extent that matter seems more real to us than energetic processes. Our mental bandwidth has been tuned to sense fast events over slow, gradual, and subtle phenomena. As a result, our sense of integration in the ecology of the planet and cosmos has suffered.

The following two chapters illustrate how this limiting condition came to be. I will focus on the past several hundred years and the specific technological control systems that have overridden preexisting temporal patterns. I will discuss some of the technologies surrounding the regulation of time and how these systems have led to the destruction of information and our spiritual impoverishment.

Chapters 2 and 3 are academically oriented. I suggest if this type of discussion does not interest you, please skim them or skip to Chapter 4, where I introduce the idea of resonant viewing.

2. Technology and Time Control

"Mass media swamps diversity. It makes every place the same. Bangkok or Tokyo or London: there's a McDonald's on one corner, a Benneton on another, a Gap across the street. Regional differences vanish. All differences vanish. In a mass-media world, there's less of everything except the top ten books, records, movies, and ideas. People worry about losing species diversity in a rain forest. But what about intellectual diversity—our most necessary resource? That's disappearing faster than trees. But we haven't figured that out, so now we're planning to put five billion people together in cyber-space."

- Ian Malcolm in *The Lost World* (Michael Crichton).

TODAY INFORMATION TECHNOLOGY IS a popular topic. While we are continually told of the advantages of information technology, there is little popular discussion of its drawbacks. This one-sided view is partly due to our lack of understanding about the dynamics of time in living systems. As a result, our society continues to rely on anachronistic efficiency—criteria based on a mechanistic, linear, world-view. This is one of the main reasons we put our faith in external technological systems. Of all these inventions, the clock may take claim as the most important.

From Natural Time to Machine Time

Ever since the invention of agriculture and the production of a food surplus, society has become increasingly preoccupied with the control of time. Whereas hunter-gatherers followed the rhythms and patterns of nature, systematic agriculture allowed societies to alter their environment by regulating food production. To control the supply and distribution of food, institutions such as formal governments, legal codes, and religions emerged. Writing and mathematics made large-scale social control possible through the rational allocation and distribution of resources: in addition to legal and military domination, astronomy and calendars were used to coordinate and synchronize social activities (Burke and Ornstein, 1995). The seven-day week revolving around the Sabbath was invented by the ancient Jews so as to formalize a day of rest. This calendar arrangement separated sacred from secular times and solidified a dispersed community. With the invention of clocks in the early middle ages, time, was regulated with even more precision. The Benedictine monks were among the first groups to use a rigid temporal order to time hourly activities by day and night (Rifkin 1987, p. 97). After the Middle Ages, hours and minutes were increasingly employed by the larger world. As ever-smaller units of

The invention of measured time changed how we live and work.

time were measured by new time-keeping technologies, clocks were used to control the labor force and economic activity in general society.

The Dictatorship of the Clock

Lewis Mumford noted that the clock, not the steam engine, was the primary machine of the industrial revolution. Time-keeping devices allowed action and motion to be stripped from a natural context and placed into an economic context. According to Jeremy Rifkin, medieval peasants had over 150 holidays a year. The flow of time was "still sporadic, leisurely, unpredictable, and above all tied to experiences rather than abstract numbers" (Rifkin, p. 101). The peasants' day was divided into three time periods: sunrise, high noon and sunset. The mechanization of time began with the rise of the merchant class who used clocks in their businesses and personal lives. By applying clocks to previously unregulated activities, the bourgeoisie of Europe implemented the mechanization of time that prevails over the planet today.

The Dictatorship of the Clock.

Whereas work had generally been task-driven, it now became oriented around schedules and time limits. The flow of time came to be measured and parceled out by machines rather than by the seasons or the movement of the sun and nature. This "rationalization" of time transformed a plethora of heterogeneous, local times into uniform, hourly zones. The new rationalized temporal system ignored actual solar time, unique at each point on the globe. The clock disconnected people from their innate biological and ecological rhythms. Where medieval craftsmen and peasants were once free to set their work schedules, they now worked under the "dictatorship of the clock." Work was dissociated from the local environment and sublimated to the dictates of a hegemonic global economic system.

Whereas in craft trades and in farming the workers had set the pace of activity, in the new factory system the machinery dictated the tempo. That tempo was incessant, unrelenting, and exacting. Industrial production mode was, above all else, methodical. Its rhythm mirrored the rhythm of the clock. The new worker was expected to surrender his time completely to the new factory rhythm. He was to show up on time, work at the pace the machine set, and then leave at the appointed time. Subjective time considerations had no place inside the factory. There, objective time—machine time—ruled supreme. (Rifkin, p. 105)

The new time order stressed punctuality and conformity. Employers controlled laborers' actions minute by minute and used the church to control time spent outside the factory. In more recent times, clock culture found its greatest supporter in Frederick Winslow Taylor's scientific management: scientific analysis was used to estimate the minimum time necessary to complete a given task. Complex tasks were broken down into rudimentary movements with the use of stop-motion photography. Scientific management eliminated any subjective aspect of work and reduced it to timed labor. Initially, there was widespread resistance by workers and a bill was even passed by Congress to prevent its implementation in the Navy and post office. Despite widespread worker turnover, hostility to scientific management and the mechanized assembly lines, this form of organization became the dominant industrial work paradigm.

Scientific management remained the leading mode of work - organization until the influence of Edward Deming in Japan after World War II. Deming stressed new management practices based on the importance of quality, rather than just the quantity of production. This led to the invention of increased flexibility in the work arrangement, with increased communications between workers and employers, as well as a more flexible work schedule. However, though less important as a management principle, the imperative of scientific management became strongly incorporated in information technologies that broke information down into its smallest parts to encode it as binary logical bits.

As a result, we live today in a "nanosecond culture," (Rifkin, 1987) and many activities in modern societies, such as email, require ever-faster response times. Virtually every social activity today is time-encoded in some way, and clocks are embedded in all types of technology. The process of rationalization has now permeated private life in addition to the work world. Everyday a bit more of our lives are mediated by machines and more of our time is subject to rational control—less and less is left to chance. "Electronic communication is an instantaneous and illusory contact that creates a sense of intimacy without the emotional investment that leads to close friendships" (Stoll, 1995, p. 26).

Complex technological connectedness can have unpredictable effects upon evolution and living systems. As the technology becomes more sophisticated, many cultural and social processes based on spatial separation and time lags lose depth and resiliency.

Scientific Management: "Time is Money."

The Standardization of Time and Space

One of the main features of modern society is the way in which time is increasingly abstracted from a natural environment and turned over to machines and clocks. The social scientist Anthony Giddens (1990) refers to this as "time-space distanciation." The idea implies that previously related events in space and time are now abstracted from their local, social, and economic contexts and reconnected on a global scale. Standardization and uniformity eventually permeate all facets of modern society. Interactions take place across spatial and temporal boundaries that had previously prevented such activity. When social institutions are "disembedded" from space and time, discontinuous interactions become commonplace. These discontinuities are seen in the pace of change, the scope of change, and the nature of modern institutions (Giddens, 1990, p. 6). Older regulatory mechanisms, cultural and institutional, are superseded by a standardized temporal and spatial control. Continuous relationships give way to interrupted interactions. These rationalized interactions are only created by abstracting natural and chaotic patterns from their local contexts to make them uniform, predictable, and controllable on a global scale. Global patterns then come to dominate local systems.

Disembedding (the abstraction of time and space from local contexts) is the primary characteristic of modernity. Where time and space are intrinsically related in pre-modern societies, abstracted precise time measurement and the standardization of social time create a separation of time and space. Time is now independent of space; distance is no longer an impediment to social interaction.

The invention of the mechanical clock and its diffusion to virtually all members of the population (a phenomenon which dates at its earliest from the late eighteenth century) were of key significance in the separation of time from space. The clock expressed a uniform dimension of "empty" time, quantified in such a way as to permit the precise designation of "zones" of the day (e.g., "the working day").

Time was still connected with space (and place) until the uniformity of time measurement by the mechanical clock was matched by uniformity in the social organization of time. This shift coincided with the expansion of modernity and was not completed until the current century (Giddens, pp. 17-8).

From this perspective, modernity is seen as a shift in humans' relationships to the rhythms of the universe.

Similarly, Rifkin argues that the control of time is a basic conflict in our history. Our increasing dependence on computers has led to a new reckoning of time, an extreme form of temporal abstraction that could have dire human consequences. The history of human technological change is marked by alterations of social temporal patterns. These changes have culminated in a world whose temporal patterns are seemingly fragmented and discontinuous:

As the tempo of modern life has continued to accelerate, we come to feel increasingly out of touch with the biological rhythms of the past, unable to experience a close connection with the natural environment. The human work time is no longer joined to the incoming and outgoing tides, the rising and setting sun and the changing seasons. Instead, humanity has created an artificial time environment punctuated by mechanical contrivances and electronic impulses: a time plane that is quantitative, fast-paced, efficient and predictable.

The modern age is characterized by a Promethean spirit, a restless energy that preys on speed records and shortcuts, unmindful of the past, uncaring of the future, existing only for the moment and the quick fix . . . Lost in a sea of perpetual technological transition, modern man and woman find themselves increasingly alienated from the ecological choreography of the planet. (Rifkin, pp. 20-1)

The rapid pace of life has created a "time famine" that threatens to make people weary and frantic. The more technology we have, the more hurried we feel (Young, 1988).

This artificial time environment cuts us off from the natural world around us. Instead, we seem increasingly tied to clock-time as opposed to natural time. The accelerated information economy, the so-called "information age," has created disconnected social interactions independent of a global temporal context: day and night are no longer seen as distinct temporal zones with different rules of social behavior. The extension of work activity into the night has led to collective social behavior whereby the distinctions between traditional work and leisure-time boundaries found in the industrial era no longer exist. Thus, new temporal rhythms based on the exigencies of electronic communication technology are rapidly replacing patterns that evolved during the industrial or agrarian era. These new rhythms, based mainly on rapid economic transactions, are creating stress and disconnection:

> . . .The features that make our economy global and nonstop also induce a pervasive human fatigue that saps creativity, performance, and drive to excel. The increasing reliance on automation and on twenty-four-hour-a-day productions pulls the most critical employees in the producing economy into a world for which their bodies were not designed. (Moore-Ede, 1993, p. 85)

Similarly, as we become increasingly plugged into a machine economy, we become alienated from our inner intelligence. We spend so much time managing fast machines that we no longer have to pay attention to the needs of our bodies and spirits. This numbing process results in cutting ourselves off from our own bodily communication systems.

The immediacy of information technology illustrates one aspect of disembedding. Today, news of worldwide events travels around the globe in minutes or seconds. Technological barriers to global communication have decreased to the point where our absorption of new information is limited by our own psychological makeup rather than the availability of information itself. Though information circulates globally, modern people and organizations suffer from a condition of "information overload" meaning more energy is put into disseminating and absorbing information than is devoted to analyzing or understanding it. Short-term events seem to take precedence over long-term events and for that reason our comprehension of the underlying dynamics of our world decreases. Thus, the increased flow of information made possible by technical improvement may be linked with our own intellectual impoverishment.

The cause of this impoverishment is straightforward: When information or knowledge is taken out of a specific context, it gains functional or technical value, but loses some of the referential significance and potential usefulness. Because knowledge formation is not a linear process, the sheer quantity of information does not make up for a loss of diversity and variability. This loss of quality is a direct result of our attempts to manipulate and control information.

Information technology is not a neutral medium, but is embedded with very selective screening mechanisms. These selective mechanisms are the outcome of the predominant temporal framework employed by social organizations. By selecting out information that easily fits into prearranged categories of coding or content, information technology destroys information (Beniger, 1986). Not only is information

Formal time-keeping systems destroy information.

excluded from the processing system, but the processed information is of transient value due to its highly specific content.

The easier it is to manipulate and move information through electronic media, the less value any given piece of information will contribute to our long-term knowledge. Many bits of short-term data and information do not necessarily coalesce into knowledge. Because of the nonlinear and complex nature of the way we think and interpret our surroundings, knowledge is an inherently interactive and a cumulative process. Yet it is precisely this natural complexity that is threatened by the dominance of mechanistic time. Information technology, by virtue of its tendency to reduce informational complexity, changes the way we think about ourselves and the world. Widespread dependence on short-term, quantifiable flows of information has unintended consequences for our development and adaptability.

Cultural Lag and Social Catastrophe

The work American sociologist Thorstein Veblen illustrates the unintended consequences of technology. In his analysis of Imperial Germany, Veblen (1915) noted the paradoxical social and political effects of rapid technological change. A speedy industrialization increased Germany's economic might, but it also created cultural and political forces that undermined the legitimacy of existing social institutions. Veblen saw Imperial Germany as an authoritarian society based on dynastic political ambitions and unquestioning subservience of its people. Yet factories and urbanized workplaces inevitably led to the growth of democratic organizations that in turn eroded existing authoritarian institutions:

Nothing short of the fullest usufruct of this technology will serve the material needs of the modern warlike State, yet the discipline incident to a sufficiently unreserved addiction to this mechanistic technology will unavoidably disintegrate the institutional foundations of such a system of to be unable to get along without the machine industry, and also, in the long run, unable to get along with it since this industrial system undermines the foundation of the State (Veblen, pp. 270-1).

Veblen implies here that Germany's dependence on technology created a contradiction between the political and industrial systems. As the latter became stronger, the former would weaken. This problematic situation did not occur in countries such as England where industrialization had been the result of the activity of the middle-class entrepreneurs over the course of two centuries. In Germany "reform from above" created an industrialized economy in only two decades; the resulting turmoil created reactionary social movements, which set the stage for the rise of the National Socialist party several decades later. Whereas in England technology arose indigenously, in Germany it was imported into the society ready-made from England. Veblen anticipated that in a democratized Germany, dynastic elites would attempt to hold on to their power and feudal privileges by resorting to warfare and internal repression.

Time used to be measured by the rhythmic cycles of day and night.

For Veblen, the rapidity of technological change in Imperial Germany was sufficient to generate social disorder and the potential for warfare. Gradual change can be assimilated; rapid technological development, however, leads to potentially violent conflict as older institutions try to retain control. This theory is the precursor to the general idea of cultural lag as popularized by American sociologist William Ogburn (1957). For Ogburn, "a cultural lag occurs when one of two parts of culture which are correlated changes before or in a greater degree than other part does, thereby causing less adjustment between the two parts than existed previously" (p. 167). This perspective rests on the assumption that technology changes faster than culture or social institutions: technology leads and culture lags. For Ogburn, these lags exist mainly in the short-term because over long periods of history the lags catchup. However, the pace of technological change appears faster in the present than in the past, and cultural lag may be more persistent now. Toffler makes similar arguments in *Future Shock* (1971) where he argues that rapidly changing technology leads to something similar to a sonic shock comparable to what supersonic airplanes experience, except on a social level.

In a related way, the rapidity with which new information technologies have been adopted in the last decade is leading to cultural lag. First, there is a newly created sense of immediacy. Previously unconnected persons and institutions can now communicate instantaneously: this is particularly true with respect to visual mass media. This sense of immediacy may lead to us to have inherent preferences for some types of knowledge over others. The process of rigidification affects information by changing its content, specifically its complexity, which is important in the evolution of biological organisms and social institutions. Second, the mechanistic control of information is likely to produce chaotic social and ecological consequences because it is in the nature of technological systems to destroy complex information. Thus, Jaques Ellul (1964) argues that "technique" is an end in itself. The technological process supersedes content as systems become routine. Technique "refers to any complex of standardized means for attaining a predetermined result. Thus, it converts spontaneous and unreflective behavior into result" (Ellul, p. vi). This form of instrumental rationality transcends the machines and devices that manifest its logic. "Technique integrates the machine into society. . . It clarifies, arranges, and rationalizes; it does in the domain of the abstract what the machine did in the domain of labor. It is efficient and brings efficiency to everything" (Ellul, p. 5).

Because of the tendency of rationalized systems toward rigidity, there is an inevitable conflict between the resources that technology transforms and the ecologically complex processes that support technological systems. These resources include not merely materials and energy in the traditional sense; they include variability and diversity. By decomposing complexity into regularity, technological systems eventually feed back upon the very resources they have created. Because regularized resources do not have the same degree of complexity as their original sources, technology becomes self-consuming, producing first a monoculture and then, perhaps, chaotic disintegration. Thus, when the medium becomes more

Industrialization changed our perception of time from one of natural rhythms to those based on mathematical measurement.

important than the message, variations in informational structure and content are dampened. Instead of helping societies to adapt and innovate in the face of social and political problems, technology can serve to conserve existing institutions. Joseph Weizenbaum, a former computer engineer at MIT, points out the institutional effects of computers:

Many of the problems of growth and complexity that pressed insistently and irresistibly for response during the postwar decades could have served as incentives for social and political innovation. An enormous acceleration of social invention, had it begun then, would now seem to us as natural a consequence of man's predicament in that time as does the flood of technological invention and innovation that was actually stimulated.

Yes, the computer did arrive "just in time." But in time for what? In time to save—and very nearly intact, indeed, to entrench and stabilize—social and political structures that otherwise might have been either radically renovated or allowed to totter under the demands that are sure to be made on them. The computer then was used to conserve America's social and political institutions. It buttressed them and immunized them, at least temporarily, against enormous pressures for change (Weizenbaum, 1976, p. 31).

This implies that, in serving to hinder institutional adaptation or transformation, technological systems risk causing the destruction of ecological complexity: When technological modes of control are employed **alternate developmental trajectories are eliminated and competing strategies are not considered.**

Ivan Illich (1973) recognized this problem, the destruction of social alternatives, in the "second watershed," a term that refers to the reification and monopolization of social services and activities by professional elites. Originally created to solve existing social problems, such institutions as the medical and educational establishments became self-serving entities processing people as if they were lifeless objects. Bureaucratic domination coupled with technological efficiency turns people into dependent consumer-addicts unable to exercise choice of free will. Society becomes imprisoned by the tools of its own construction.

At first, new knowledge is applied to the solution of a clearly stated problem, and scientific measuring sticks are applied to account for the new efficiency. But at a second point, the progress demonstrated in a previous achievement is used as a rationale for the exploitation of society as a whole in the service of a value which is determined and constantly revised by an element of society, by its self-certifying elites. Ivan Illich illustrates this idea as follows:

In the case of transportation it has taken almost a century to pass from an era served by motorized vehicles to the era in which society has been reduced to virtual enslavement to the car. During the American Civil War, steam power on wheels became effective. The new economy in transportation enabled many people to travel by rail at the speed of a royal coach, and to do so with a comfort kings had not dared dream of. Gradually, desirable locomotion was associated and finally identified with high vehicular speeds. But when transportation had passed through its second watershed, vehicles had created more distances than they helped to bridge; more time was used by the entire society for the sake of traffic than was "saved" (Illich, p. 8).

The ossification of technological systems serves to reinforce the power of existing elites and reduce the freedom of the society as a whole by eliminating alternatives. The latest development of information technologies may serve as precursor to a second watershed in the control of time. Though efficient in some realms, the ever-pervasive application of these technologies may simply serve to establish mechanisms for micromanaging previously spontaneous actions and processes.

In our attempt to control previously unregulated resources, we are setting in motion irreversible processes with unforeseen consequences. Far from making our world more orderly and peaceful, the opposite may be occurring. Agrarian societies improved food-producing techniques, while industrialized societies found new ways to use chemicals, metals, and energy sources. Greater regulation of information allowed modern society to increase its control over an ever-expanding network of systems. If societies understood the consequences of their control at each stage of development, this new knowledge could be applied to later periods of evolution. However, the theory of cultural lag postulates that societies' cultures and values never catch up with technological change. Institutions and mentalities that do not fit are repressed, removed, or modified in one form or another until only a monoculture remains. This whole evolutionary process is inherently chaotic and limited as demonstrated by the energy that was available for war and conflict used by Germany's Third Reich.

Each successive technological paradigm has consequences that make the development of the next generation of technology a necessity. The agrarian revolution, by allowing for more food production by fewer agriculturalists, created the conditions that fostered the development of an artisan class, urban areas, centralized political power, and permanent armies. Industrialization created mountains of formal information and new information technologies provided the means to keep track of the increasing production and distribution of goods and services. As they inevitably feed back into the systems which created them, all technologies eventually create other problems and a demand for new solutions. When the gap between these needs and existing institutions is large, then large-scale social reorganization and unforeseen paradigm shifts are more likely to happen.

In our time, new quantum technologies are arising that will extend the capacity for communication and computation in untold ways. However, it is clear that systems based on sub-atomic principles will exacerbate these paradigm shifts even further.

Technology, Complexity, and Chaos

Technological systems constrain natural variability, diversity, and complexity. In general, the complexity of a local area is reduced by a technological system's control of social and natural resources; the more things are controlled, the more they are made increasingly uniform and homogenous. Ultimately, this transformational process results in systemic reification such that diversity and spontaneity are permanently diminished. Thus, as technology solves one set of problems, it creates others.

Excessive control inevitably results in "surprises:" chaotic activity that originates from within the system itself (Holling, 1986). So external technology tends to increase complexity and chaos simultaneously. On the other hand, if flexibility and ambiguity were allowed, the overall system would be more resilient to change: global variations would be less likely to lead to irreversible, paradigmatic changes in systems where local stability is rigidly maintained. Quantum technologies offer this possibility.

Today, discontinuities in our social and economic systems are coming from places never before taken seriously in our collective thinking. Yet the evidence is clear that new means of subtle energy communications are enabling the average person to bypass the technological systems all around them and directly connect to a more universal form of information flow. In effect, the very systems that have provided the Western world with a high standard of living and economic abundance are undermining the very ideological foundations that produced these benefits in the first place. Thus the chaotic dynamics that are increasingly affecting our society are produced from within and are generating ever more powerful shock waves in our consciousness. These waves promise to overturn our most fundamental beliefs about the universe and our role in it.

3. The Age of Missing Information:

The Paradox of Efficiency and Effectiveness

ONE OF THE MAIN points I've picked up from my study of time is that mechanistic technologies are also associated with limiting belief systems predicated on the idea of scarcity within ourselves and our environment. This artificial scarcity that we have adopted as a collective ideology leads us to increasingly rely on external processes instead of internal processes. While we place less faith in our spiritual selves, we displace that faith to machines and bureaucratic organizations that administer them. Thus as a trade-off for organizing our lives around these complex technologies and organizations over the course of several centuries, the patterns of human life have ceased to be embedded in the rhythms of the planet and the local environment.

How Our Collective Belief Systems Created an Iron Cage

Our dependency on complex technology is in part due to our collective belief systems. At the turn of the century, the German sociologist Max Weber described some of these issues in terms of what he called "instrumental rationality," whereby everything is subject to quantitative calculation. For Weber, the rationalization of social life and the dominance of instrumental rationality was a central feature of Western civilization. In our own time, information technologies represent an extension of instrumental rationality to new spheres of life previously outside the realm of technical control.

Therefore, the effects of the rationalization of information were similar to other types of technological change in the past century.

Weber described many of his ideas about the forces leading to the rationalization of Western culture in *The Protestant Ethic and the Spirit of Capitalism* (1958). Modern capitalism, Weber argued, is the historical outcome of the actions of people who held the Protestant ethic at the core of their belief system. In contrast to Catholicism, Protestantism contained a set of values and social norms conducive to an economic system based on individual achievement and success. Where Catholicism had allowed personal salvation through confession and atonement, Protestantism maintained that one had a direct relationship with God. Luther's idea of the "calling" (*Beruf*) transformed other-worldly asceticism into vocational asceticism, an outlook emphasizing duty in everyday life. The Calvinist doctrine added the idea of predestination to the Protestant ethic: one could not know his destiny despite its predetermination by God. This judgment was seen in material signs of success, hints from the divine of personal salvation or damnation in the afterlife. Thus the Protestant Ethic and the personal habits it entailed are rational methods for gaining information about the afterlife, a traditional belief. The perfectibility of man through knowledge, an idea that grew in importance during the Enlightenment, was achieved in Protestantism by way of vocational asceticism. Bound to a frugal and disciplined lifestyle, people's central preoccupation was to gain information about their fate in the afterlife.

Feeling nervous about their personal future, Protestants suffered from permanent anxiety. Daily life became a means to know one's eternal destiny. Signs of salvation were found in personal fortune and material abundance. Increasingly, people's personal habits began to resemble those of the monks': they became preoccupied with their daily routines, punctuality, and frugality. Thus, when these values escaped from the monastery into everyday life, a new economic system came into formation, one that was consistent with the actions and activities of those preoccupied with their fates. Although these modes of existence had been present in other societies, it faced the opposition of traditionalism before becoming the dominant economic mode in the West. In a traditional, pre-capitalist economy, common people worked to maintain a stable subsistence level rather than to accumulate as much as possible. Employers found that adjusting wages simply led people to work more or fewer hours to keep their earnings the same.

In modern societies, work took on a new meaning and economic activity became more oriented to promote increased wealth through accumulation. Capitalism, a system oriented toward individual achievement, became a means by which anxious persons could find signs of success. Calculated, imper

Capitalism replaced natural work rhythms with calculated, impersonal activity

sonal action motivated by a preoccupation with efficiency produced a new set of social values and organization. Social life in capitalist societies became impersonal and calculated; it eradicated the norms of egalitarianism and fraternity inherent in most religions, especially in the Judeo-Christian ethic, and replaced them with ideas of maximization and efficiency.

Thus, modern Western societies were paradoxical: the very economic values and modes of action, which led to their world supremacy, also eroded the social and religious values on which they were based. Instrumental rationality had become the predominant form of social action in the West, losing all its original religious significance. No longer connected with eternal salvation, calculated rational action came to dominate all spheres of human life, both public and private.

The "light cloak" of religious belief had become an "iron cage" in which scientific, specialized knowledge dominated traditional or spiritual modes of existence. In a world where nothing was left to chance, the pervasive rationalization of society led to "disenchant-ment," the erosion of moral values and the dissolution of traditional forms of social control. When un-provable, non-empirical traditional beliefs are displaced or subsumed by formal rationality, and life loses all but technical significance.

The Bureaucratization of Knowledge

A consequence of formal rationality was the growth of bureaucracy. Bureaucratic organization differed from other forms of social life in that it was objective, hierarchical, continuous, and permanent. Public officials, in contrast to kings' personal advisers in earlier societies, now had highly delimited spheres of competence, fixed salaries, and were accountable to a specific set of rules (Weber, 1978, pp. 956-963). Although bureaucracies existed in other societies like ancient China and Egypt, they differed from contemporary bureau-cracies in the West in that the latter were rationalized: the actions and organization of public officials were circumscribed and con-trolled by a legal system, not the personal whims of the ruler. This legalistic basis is the source of modern bureaucracies' objective and impersonal character.

Rationalization was a powerful force in modern societies. Instrumental rationality was a mode of social action in which tradition and sentiment had no place. In contrast to many thinkers such as the German philosophers, Kant and Hegel, (who believed that the application of human reason created new types of freedom and social interaction) Weber believed that instrumental rationality eroded the very foundations that gave it birth. With its emphasis on individuals' rational actions, this new ethos destroyed concern for social welfare and shared values. The decline of traditional social control was not only dangerous in that it deprived individuals of feeling that their lives were inherently meaningful or worthwhile; bureaucratic organizations became increasingly guided by more narrow perspectives, goals, and more specialized scientific knowl-edge.

Losing a broader social purpose, organizations became guided by specialized experts who had no other interest than in preserving and extending their personal power. Weber suggested that where knowledge threatens to disrupt bureaucracies' operations, bureaucrats and experts would sabotage public inquiry. Societies guided by purely instrumental means became dominated by bureaucratic institutions run by "specialists without spirit, sensualists without soul" (Weber, 1958, p. 182). Bureaucracies turned into technocracies that thrived on narrow, self-serving goals. Instrumental rationality erodes the values that gave rise to it in the first place and replaces those ideas with more narrow efficiency criteria. Thus all types of activities tend to get measured in terms of productivity, speed, and predictability.

The industrial revolution led to a crisis of control

Industrialization and The Crisis of Control

While bureaucratic organization originated in ancient and modern governments, it later spread to an industrial form of organizational industry. The industrial revolution first began in England with small-to-medium scale businesses. Industrialization then spread to Germany, France, and the United States and took a unique form in each country. Despite differing social and economic forms, industrial techniques were characterized by uniform, systematic methods of production that led to rapid increases in the output of manufactured goods. The large-scale mass manufacturing created new problems in the coordination and control of production, distribution, and consumption of products. Efforts to manage this mass of information led to the "Control Revolution" (Beniger, 1986).

Just as the industrial revolution was based on advances in agriculture, increasing dependence on industrial technology demanded better methods of accounting, calculation, and communication. The very success of the industrial revolution led to a "crisis of control" where increasing production outstripped existing business organizations' ability to keep track of their operation. As industrial societies became more differentiated and specialized, there was a need for new means of communication between increasingly isolated socioeconomic spheres (Durkheim, 1956). While pre-modern societies were based on face-to-face contact, industrial societies lacked sufficient normative integration because of the relative functional autonomy of their components (Beniger, p. 11). Similarly, large-scale, steam-driven industrial production radically changed the way materials and energy were used, and this called for new means of managing information. Traditional bureaucratic organization alone could no longer cope with the quantities of information that needed to be managed in a system of mass-production. Thus, initially, reliance on information technology was the direct outcome of the needs of an industrial society.

Devices such as the telegraph (1830s), rotary power printing (1840s), typewriter (1860s), telephone (1876), radio (1906), and television (1923) initially revolutionized human communications (Beniger, p. 7). These types of technology increased the flow of information and changed how our society interacts on all levels. Information, then content, became a function of its medium. In other words, the content was altered to fit the technology. In some cases, this meant reducing the contents' quality.

During the American Civil War, for example, newspaper articles became written in a pyramid format: The most important information was placed at the beginning of the story because of the unreliability of telegraphs. Newspapers continue to use this style because of social convention, not technical efficiency. Similarly, both radio and television had unique program lengths (half-hour or hourly) and contents (program type)—each media adapted information accordingly.

Thus, quantity of transmission in each system was achieved at the expense of changing the quality of the content. New temporal restrictions placed limitations on length of information flows and centralization of broadcast facilities allowed private networks and regulatory agencies, mainly the Federal Communications Commission, to control the content.

The Impact of Temporal Acceleration

More recently, newspaper journalism has adopted the format of tabloid TV programs. This form of "telejournalism" (Schachtman, 1995, pp. 116-117) makes newspapers subject to the same structural distortions as television where there is a tendency to: emphasize visual over written content; personalize issues and identify them with particular people such as celebrities; and focus on tabloid stories over long-term issues. To attract more readers, newspapers have tended to adopt the same low standards as television. The end result is not intelligent discussion of the issues, but "conversational narcissism" (Schachtman, p.184). This preoccupation with the short-term is not limited to journalism, but is seen in many aspects of modern life. As technology has become increasingly complex and widespread, the temporal patterns of life have ceased to be embedded in the rhythms of the planet and instead are enmeshed with the needs of technological systems. This temporal acceleration has led us to feel increasingly out of touch with large-scale processes, both biological and ecological rhythms, and unable to experience a close connection with the natural environment. As a result, we have a lot of communications power, but little real value to communicate. "Thanks to the high success of information theory, we live in a time when the technology of human communications has advanced at blinding speed: but what people have to say to one another by way of that technology shows no comparable development" (Roszak, 1994, p 16).In contrast, subtle energy technologies work by spontaneously integrating many components into one seamless flow. Because they work without a rigid distinction between means and ends, the content produced by these soft "systems" tends to be aligned with the environments they work within. They neither destroy information nor do they mold it to fit the needs of the pre-existing system. Rather the system evolves concomitantly with the information itself.

However, electronic information technologies tend to modify content. In the same manner that bureaucracies serve to simplify and depersonalize the management of people and resources, information technologies systematize, filter, and routinize the management of information. In this way, information technology acts similarly to bureaucracy. Efficiency, impersonality, and an objective orientation characterize both the operations of bureaucracies and computers. Also, the way in which both serve to control information is very similar: increasing quantities of information are managed by rationalizing them to fit into the structure of these systems.

Bureaucracies and computers can make us feel alienated and irrelevant

Although the term has a variety of meanings, both in Weber's writings and in the elaborations of his work by others, most definitions are subsumed by one essential idea: control can be increased not only by increasing the capability to process information, but also by decreasing the amount of information to be processed. The former approach to control was realized in Weber's day through bureaucratization; today it is increasingly realized through computerization.

By means of rationalization, therefore, it is possible to maintain large-scale, complex social systems that would be overwhelmed by a rising tide of information they could not process were it necessary to govern by the particularistic considerations of family and kin that characterize pre-industrial societies.

*In short, rationalization might be defined as the destruction or
ignoring of information in order to facilitate its processing*
(Beniger, p. 15, my emphasis).

The rationalization of information, then, has a similar character in
all types of information processing systems. Information
technologies, both organizational and technical, serve to preserve
existing hierarchies by reducing the complexity of their
environments. Both bureaucratic organizations and information
processing systems, in an attempt to control their
environments, destroy or reduce their complexity.

Historically, complexity reduction is an important aspect of
rationalization and the developments that led to the creation of the
"information age." These included global time zones, standardized
forms and grading, fixed prices, and trademarks. Time zones, as
noted in the previous chapter, served to standardize national and
international commercial transactions, science, and railroads. The
rationalization of time in this way transformed a plethora of
heterogeneous, local times and transformed them into uniform,
hourly zones. The new rationalized temporal system ignored actual
solar time, unique at each point on the globe. Complex, non-
quantifiable information was lost in this simplified "preprocessing"
system (Beniger, p.16).

The standardization of world time marked the final victory
for efficiency. Local times had long been tied to traditional
values, nature, the gods, and the mythic past. The new
world time was bound only to abstract numbers. It flowed
evenly and remained aloof and detached from parochial
interests. The new time was expressed only as a single
dimension: utility. The industrial nations adopted a
universal standardized time frame simply because it was
more efficient. The world was being readied for the new
temporal imperialism.

It took six hundred years to revolutionize the temporal orientation of Europe. It took only one-third that time to extend the temporal revolution to countries and cultures across the globe. In the sixteenth, seventeenth, and eighteenth centuries, European armies colonized the territories of the planet. In the nineteenth and twentieth centuries, European and American industry colonized the time frame of much of the rest of the world (Rifkin, 1987, p. 134).

The standardization of time was one prerequisite for industrialization and mass production. Work life was disassociated from the rhythms of organic life allowing for the control of labor in ever more rigorous ways. The success of industrial production eventually let it to exceed the ability of existing systems to keep track of the production, distribution, and consumption of goods and services. New means of information processing were needed to manage these increasing flows. Rationalization, therefore, is an all-encompassing process that affects interactions and events beyond its immediate sphere of application. As shown

Does technology give us more time? Or simply place us on a faster running "techno-time?"

below, it is not a singular event but a dynamic that creates unintended consequences never anticipated by its architects.

Is Faster Always Better?
Among recent works that portend the coming of a new "information age," Alvin Toffler's *Powershift* (1990) is a good example of this

perspective's view of future societal development. The central thesis of this perspective is that knowledge is being increasingly substituted for material resources, energy, and time. New modes of interaction, made possible by the computer and information technology, alter the bases of institutions' power. Older hierarchical organizations are falling in the face of new institutions based on horizontally-structured networks. This networked, global economy will generate wealth from services, knowledge, and symbolic resources. In this new era, power is shifting away from centralized empires and moving towards corporations and individuals that have access to immediate and specialized exchange of information. "Knowledge is power" is the motto of the "powershift era." Toffler identifies the simultaneity of interactions permitted by complex electronic information systems as an agent of this momentous change. Information flows at faster rates in an accelerated information economy than in

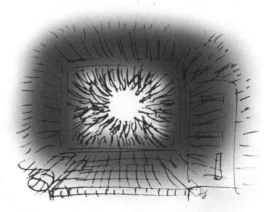

Technology can destroy information.

an industrial economy. Intermediaries are no longer necessary in a world where horizontal networks surpass bureaucracies in their efficiency and speed. From this perspective, the speed of technological interactions is all-important. There is no attention paid to integration and balance as a component of social and personal well-being.

Another perspective comes from Winner (1986) who argues that the spread of electronic information systems reinforces existing social relations and organizations by strengthening those who already possess power: large-scale technological systems have a conservative effect on society. This idea is similar to Weizenbaum's (1976) claim that historically computers have dampened social and economic change. Not a true substitute for face-to-face contact, telecommunications creates an illusion of democratic participation. Effective contestation, an important component of democratic societies, is supplanted by benign conformity to the imperatives of electronic devices. Current developments in the information age suggest an increase in power by those who already had a great deal of power, an enhanced centralization of control, by those already prepared for control and an augmentation of wealth by the already wealthy. Far from demonstrating a revolution in patterns of social and political influence, empirical studies of computers and social change usually show powerful groups adapting computerized methods to retain control (Winner, p. 107).

A recent book, *IBM and the Holocaust* by Edwin Black (2001), makes a similar point. If it were not for computer punch cards and the means to sort and analyze them, Hitler would not have able to carry out his genocidal plans. In the case of the Nazi's extermination of select minority groups, computers allowed them to identify millions of targeted people and administer the records of those destined for concentration camps.

A second important issue related to accelerated flows of information is its short-lived quality: the more immediate the information, the more specific its context of application. Therefore, greater flows of information do not necessarily translate into increased knowledge production; the opposite case may be true. This paradox results from the previously discussed phenomenon: the formal rationality of technical means destroys the substantive value of the ends. Knowledge is produced through the cognitive synthesis of information over the long-term. If information becomes increasingly transient and context specific, synthesis is less likely to occur and less knowledge is created. Thus, the acceleration of information flows in recent decades and new standards of immediacy created by the news media stifle the development of new ideas.

Information processing systems function by destroying or ignoring raw information and its context. In the quest for greater levels of efficiency and processing speed, complexity is transformed into simplicity. Thus, the very immediacy of information systems alters the contextual, relational nature of knowledge. The creation of knowledge is an inherently dialectical, nonlinear process; Toffler and others incorrectly suggest that accelerated information flows will create more knowledge, therefore greater social power. Specifically, the widespread availability of various types of information, technical facts, or personal communication available to individuals does not by itself ensure that new ideas or knowledge will be used.

Modern organizations are continually faced with overload, a flood of data that threatens to become unintelligible to them. Computers provide one way to confront that problem; speed conquers quantity. An equally serious challenge is created by the fact that the varieties of information most crucial to modern organizations are highly time specific. Data on stock market prices, airline traffic, weather conditions, international economic indicators, military intelligence, public opinion poll results, and the like are useful for very short periods of time. Systems that gather, organize, analyze, and utilize electronic data in these areas must be closely tuned to the very latest development . . . Information about prices an hour old or even a few seconds old may have no value. Information is itself a perishable commodity (Winner, pp. 113-4).

The value of information is temporally specific: Lacking a specific context it cannot be synthesized into knowledge, let alone wisdom. Yet the rapidity and instantaneous nature of accelerated information threatens to overload the temporal capacity of humans who evolved in the presence of less hurried yet more rhythmically complex biological and ecological patterns. Thus while speed may increase quantity, it is not a substitute for quality—informational complexity is not simply the product of aggregated, microscopic bits of information. Preoccupied with efficiency criteria, however, electronic information systems reduce complexity and erode the substantive meaning of information.

The agronomist Wes Jackson (1987) makes a similar argument in his views about technology and farming: the extinction of species, genetic monocultures, and the depopulation of rural areas (all partly caused by the rise of large-scale agribusiness) are leading to an information implosion. Age-old farming knowledge and traditions are disappearing before the onslaught of modern agricultural production. The increase in formal technical knowledge has been achieved at the expense of informal, traditional farming culture learned from generations of experience and hardship. Biological diversity in crops and livestock has been reduced to a few high-yield varieties. Where rural areas once served as depositories for cultural wisdom, modern technological systems have turned them into productively efficient yet culturally lacking—corporate monocultures (Shiva 1997). Echoing Holling's concerns (1986), Jackson warns that the monopoly of formal knowledge and techniques threatens the resiliency of ecosystems.

Similarly, Raeburn's study of modern agriculture methods (1995) shows that the quest to produce uniform, unblemished fruits and vegetables has led to a dangerously high level of genetic uniformity in agricultural crops. While yields of corn, tomatoes, and wheat have increased greatly since 1930, the risk of crop failure to lack of genetic diversity has also risen, creating a greater probability for famine (p. 37). The agricultural industry is also controlled by fewer and larger companies that regulate seed supply. Environmental threats combined with less genetic adaptability mean that our food supply is increasingly vulnerable to disturbances.

Recent evidence also demonstrates that high yield crops grown in the Third World under the auspices of the Green Revolution are contributing to malnutrition and poor health. High yield crops were developed with quantity in mind, and many crops lack sufficient amounts of iron, zinc, and vitamin A (*New Scientist,* March 30, 1996). In addition to the expense of fertilizers and pesticides, genetically manipulated high-yield crops also contribute to widespread vitamin and mineral deficiencies in developing countries.

These developments are not the random outcome of misinformed agricultural policy, but the end consequence of an economically rationalized mind set. This *Weltanschauung* (worldview) believes that:

> . . . a farm or a forest is or ought to be the same as a factory; that care is only minimally necessary in the use of the land; that affection is not necessary at all; that for all practical purposes a machine is as good as a human; that the industrial standards of production, efficiency, and profitability are the only standards that are necessary; that the topsoil is lifeless and inert; that soil biology is safely replaceable by soil chemistry; that the nature of ecology of any given place is irrelevant to the use of it; that there is no value in human community or neighborhood; and that technological innovation will produce only benign results. (Berry, p. 13, 1987)

This phenomenon of viewing everything in simplistic economic terms creates the conditions for the pervasiveness of Gresham's law—"as long as it's fast, bad software drives out good" (Stoll, p. 67).

These examples consistently show a pattern in modern life whereby we sacrifice quality for quantity. Where efficiency has become the predominant criterion of evaluating an activity, something else is always lost in the process, be it informational depth, the nutritional value of food, or the genetic diversity of crops. In short, where principles of scientific management are employed, an "information implosion" results, destroying long-term cumulative memory. Where the flow of resources has been accelerated, the amount of resiliency, depth, and diversity diminishes at a local level. This historical relationship is so widespread in the modern world that it is worth paying attention to: complex technology, employed at global scales, appears inseparably linked to the degeneration of self-organizing systems.

Another issue that arises from accelerated information flows is the loss of social and cultural identity. Humans derive their sense of identity from the spatial and temporal boundaries that contain them. The interaction between people and their environments is bounded by temporal and spatial contexts. Social structure is in part a function of synchronistic activity enabled by routine, regularized, temporal patterns. Some types of events are irregular or spontaneous while others are cyclical and long-term. A dependency on fast-cycling variables entailed by the pervasive computerization of society may undermine the slower ecological components. The decline of bureaucracy in the wake of horizontally connected social units, as cited by Toffler, is but one example of this phenomenon.

Technology can cause stress on our physiology.

Yet, in some circumstances, slowness may have advantages over speed: the predominance of fast-cycling variables may have undesirable consequences on knowledge formation and unforeseeable effects on social and cultural identity. "Human beings and human societies . . . have traditionally found their identities within spatial and temporal limits. They have lived, acted, and found meaning in a particular place at a particular time. Developments in microelectronics tend to dissolve these limits, thereby threatening the integrity of social and political forms that depend on them" (Winner, p. 116).

Thus there is tension between rationalization and cultural identity, an issue not fully examined by proponents of the information age. Though accelerated flows of information may increase technical and (perhaps) organizational efficiency over the long-term, the social implications are uncertain. Though it may be a solution to problems created through mass production, the information age also has unwanted or undesirable outcomes.

Eliminating Informational Diversity

The destruction of information by electronic processing systems illustrates a central characteristic of technology; namely, that complex heterogeneous resources are transformed into simplified and uniformed standardized flows. For example, McKibben (1992) argues that with cable television "we can find subjects of interest to all only by *erasing* content, paring away information . . ." (p. 48). This reductionism is true of many types of technologies. Fluctuations of energy and information are transformed into homogenized and predictable processes. When complex rhythmic structures are dampened, information is lost:

> The relentless flood of information we receive, then, does not necessarily equal an understanding of our situation. The principal boast of electronic communication is speed, and speed doesn't help much in grasping these situations—it doesn't matter if you learn about the greenhouse effect this week or next week or next month. What matters is that when you do hear about it you understand it so deeply and thoroughly that you begin to question the way you live. (McKibben, p.162)

Schachtman, for example, reports that the number of words used by news broadcasters has declined from about 10,000 in 1960s to about 7,500 today (pp. 122-124). Sentences are also becoming less complex. The mass media lack real thinking and serve more to manipulate and control audiences rather than to inform them. In news, for example, "Correspondents . . . who are capable of sustained reflection and analysis, have no opportunities to apply those journalistic tools because they are serving principally as funnels for quotes from officials" (Schachtman, p. 129).

The temporal rationalization of modern societies, characterized by standardized temporal sequences, durations, and rhythms, yields questionable outcomes, specifically with regard to destruction of knowledge and information. In his study of technology and warfare, Van Crevald (1990) concludes that the development of high-tech fighting and communications equipment and the increased use of computers has been detrimental to the conduct of warfare. While technology has improved the coordination, timing, and management of one's forces, the very linearity inherent in sophisticated technical systems is a strategic disadvantage. Whereas technological systems are based on predictability, effective military strategy demands a high degree of ambiguity:

> ... by increasing predictability, technology reduces uncertainty: this gives more useful information to one's opponent. Thus, the very efficiency criteria that are so highly valued in some spheres of modern society are a discreet disadvantage in another. Since technology and war operate on a logic which is not only different but opposed, nothing is less conducive to victory in war than to wage it on technological principles (p. 319).

The main point here is that mechanistically structured systems do not have the inherent flexibility of self-organized ones. Over-centralization and bureaucratic command serve to degenerate the value of our time and information. Computers, administration, and communications often lead to a state of over quantification whereby everything has to be numerically measured. Yet, as I will show below, many subtle energy processes are not easily subject to precise quantification. Their existence is beyond doubt. Therefore, we should not be so quick to elevate quantified information at the cost of the more subtle types.

Fuzzy Systems

The idea that efficiency can diminish effectiveness can be generalized to many aspects of living systems, such as language, that are inherently ambiguous (Zeleny 1991). The meaning of a particular piece of information is dependent on the listener who receives it. Zeleny points out that words like *tall, young,* and *high* are indefinite apart from a specific context. Linguistic notions alone cannot be reduced to simplified meanings. Communication processes depend on the experiences of both the speaker and listener: the meaning of a particular set of words or phrases is not independent of the participants. "Knowledge refers to the overall network configuration of these concepts, not to any of its particular components" (p. 370). As language is a negotiated process, it depends on the social context of speakers and listeners.

The richer and more reliable the shared knowledge and experience, the less precise (and more "fuzzy") the information transmitting utterance can be. Much more complicated and much more precise utterances have to be constructed when there is little or no preexisting knowledge shared or assumed. Taken in its requisite context, a fuzzy utterance can therefore be as or even more precise than a "precise" utterance. An ambiguous wink of the eye, "uttered" in its proper context, can transmit more information, more reliably and more precisely, than a mathematically reasoned discourse on the desirability of certain knowledge (Zeleny, p. 366).

This view of knowledge and language lends credence to the idea that the rationalization of information exchanges quality for efficiency. As information is stripped from its context, the general "network configuration" may be lost, compromising its complexity and value. The consequences of this reductionism are widely manifested: recent catastrophes such as Bhopal, Chernobyl, and the space shuttle Challenger, show the potential consequences of dependence on narrow streams of rationalized information.

From Mechanization to Quantum Entanglement

The mechanization of time has led to the globalization of one uniform standard of time. Thus, the imperialism of formal rationality and the spread of the information technology go hand in hand. However, information technology in itself does not increase the amount of information available to us—just the opposite. The process of rationalization erases the non-quantifiable, informal, subjective information from our everyday discourse. The standardization of our life process simultaneously makes things like the Internet possible; it also causes the erosion of traditional knowledge and cultural schemes. The processes of rationalization introduce fragility into systems by eroding the integrity of fundamental institutions, increasing their brittleness and volatility.

When non-rationalized information is thrown out, highly integrated, fast-paced systems become less resilient to shocks and disturbances. The immediate gains of technology must be weighed against this loss of resiliency. Intensive manipulation of fast variables may temporarily prevent system discontinuities, but at increasingly higher costs. Societies are hindered from preventing these discontinuities as they are preoccupied with maintaining and coping with existing technological systems. As Weber foresaw, when people and organizations become narrowly focused on instrumental goals, they cease to question existing procedures and techniques and are unable to conceive of alternate courses of action. Dependent on a more narrow range of information mediums, societies may also lose the ability to use more complex resources. In a fast-paced climate of confusion, complex and contextual knowledge loses its significance. In a society based on ever accelerating interactions, instantaneous information becomes the only acceptable currency.

The control of temporal rhythms, their abstraction from biophysical contexts, and the manipulation and destruction of information by electronic processing systems—all for the sake of efficiency—are parallel processes: they are attempts to control nature and reinforce our belief in the primacy of material reality. Although this evolutionary process has led to phenomenal gains in productivity and sheer technological understanding, it has other long-term effects, such as decreased organizational effectiveness. The more systems are maintained or regulated according to short-term predictability and other efficiency criteria, the greater the potential loss of the system's ability to effectively respond to challenges and problems outside the realm of existing paradigms. Over time, internal and external disturbances become increasingly likely to shatter these brittle structures.

And yet into the cracks of this old paradigm has stepped a new set of beliefs based on very different precepts. The "Quantum Perspective" is becoming increasingly widespread, challenging the viability of our older viewpoints. As we shall see in subsequent chapters, it is precisely the ambiguity of natural information systems that allows them to transcend existing space-time boundaries and identify non-local information sources. Systems that evolve spontaneously and naturally have inherent advantages over those that don't. In contrast to the reduction of complexity that is the hallmark of mechanistic systems, quantum principles permit human-based information systems to not only increase informational quality, but to connect with subtle energies and completely new phenomena. Therefore, the rest of the book will focus not on the destruction of information, but on methodologies that preserve the fidelity of information and also bring people into contact with entirely new dimensions of life.

Part II. **Channels of Communication**

4. **Resonant Viewing:**
The Quietest Voice, the Deepest River

IN CONTRAST TO SYSTEMS that mechanistically destroy information, quantum systems use nature's information super-highway to access non-local data. Rather than fit the information into a preexisting structure, quantum systems, such as resonant viewing (described below as remote viewing), modify the human sensory-acquisition system to fit the information flows.

The Military's Secret Psychic-Viewing Program

The U.S. military's interest in remote viewing (RV) dates back to the cold war and the Soviet Union's long-time interest in psychic research, which they labeled "psychotronics." The Soviet's main interest was to psychically affect something or someone at a distance. The U. S. military felt that if the Russians had it, we had to have it too. In an apparent synchronicity, research was being conducted by Hal Puthoff and Russell Targ at Stanford Research Institute (SRI) in Palo Alto, California, into the nature of psychic perception, just as an interest was developing in the Pentagon: the military was interested in finding out if a means existed to shield itself from Soviet psychic espionage. Lieutenant Colonel Frederick Holmes "Skip" Atwater, who was involved in Pentagon security, happened to read about Puthoff and Targ's work and set out to discover if such a psychic defense system could be established. While it was eventually determined that this idea was not possible with existing technology, it did start a long-term interest in operational psychic work that was to last for over two decades and through four presidential administrations.

During this period, the U. S. Army's remote viewing unit, under the guise of the Defense Intelligence Agency and housed at Fort Meade, did work for numerous government agencies, including the Central Intelligence Agency, the Drug Enforcement Agency, and the Department of State, among others. One of the most famous successful uses of the RV unit was when president Jimmy Carter called upon one of its psychics to find a downed Soviet plane in Africa. Of course, as many of the viewing projects were classified, we still do not know what all of them entailed. However, the unit's viewers testify today that the same agencies came back repeatedly for the unit's special brand of intelligence information.

One of the major innovations in viewing research at the time was the invention of written protocols by artist and natural psychic Ingo Swann (www.BioMindSuperPowers.com). Working at SRI, Swann developed what was to be known as "coordinate remote viewing," which allowed a viewer to view anything, not just objects in boxes, as was originally the case. Swann and his colleagues found that simply by assigning a random number to a person, place, thing, or event, a trained viewer could successfully describe that target. Though other methods were used, this system, known simply as *coordinate remote viewing* (CRV), became the basis for the military's program. For a more complete history of this subject, readers are referred to Jim Schnabel's book, *Remote Viewers: The Secret History of America's Psychic Spies (1997)*, and Jim Marr's *Psi Spies* (2000).

While remote viewing is not new, some of the most famous religious figures in our history seem to have been natural "RVers." The idea that anyone can learn to do this is a new concept in the West. The military program was, in a weird way, like a spin-off from the space program, such as the artificial orange juice Tang. After the military program shut down in 1995, many of the participants in the secret program, such as Lyn Buchanan (www.CRViewer.com) and Paul Smith (www.RViewer.com), began to teach these techniques publicly. And while the techniques themselves were never classified, the whole subject still had an aura of mystery around it.

In January of 1996, I spontaneously decided to turn the radio to Boulder's local community radio station, KGNU. It was about 9 a. m. I heard a man named Dr. Courtney Brown talking about remote viewing. At this time I had never heard about the subject before: it was entirely new to me. I listened in fascination as Courtney said it was something that anyone could do, a built-in ability to perceive and accurately describe things from a distance. It had been originally designed for the military to use in the application of psychic espionage. Moreover, with this skill a person could perceive anything, including extraterrestrials and ghosts. Courtney said that what the Earth needed now were galactic ambassadors to the universe. I became intrigued with what I heard and shortly thereafter bought Brown's book, *Cosmic Voyage* (1996). This book contained some of the more interesting viewing sessions that Brown had done with his mentor (who he identified as retired military participant Ed Dames) serving as the monitor. These sessions covered everything from historical targets on Earth to the activity of different types of extraterrestrial species from around the universe.

Courtney had set up his own viewing institute in Atlanta, Georgia near Emory University where he worked in the political science department. At the Farsight Institute (www.FarSight.org), an organization that he set up in conjunction with his publisher, Courtney and an assistant taught courses in remote viewing. He believed these techniques had a lot to offer average people in terms of expanding their perceptions. At the back of Courtney's book was a telephone number for the institute and part way through the book, I called it. Courtney returned my call a few hours later and said he had one space left out of eight in the next class of May '96. The cost was $3,000, which seemed expensive, but he guaranteed results. This was to be his second class at the institute.

The course lasted eight days and was quite a mind-opening experience. Starting with simple targets, we rapidly progressed to more complex and sophisticated exercises moving around in time and space. The techniques were fairly similar to those developed by Ingo Swann, though they were more overtly structured. In Courtney's system, the protocols were designed to give the viewer a more specific idea of what he should be paying attention to at any given point in the session. In Ingo's system, the viewer was more in control, with the monitor playing only a minor role in helping the viewer to sense her perceptions. Nonetheless, most of us in the class achieved results beyond our expectations and soon we were all hooked on RV.

The remote viewing system created at the Stanford Research Institute in the 1970s was designed to be used by anyone, not just a natural psychic. The idea was that the government's intelligence services would be able to use anyone for psychic espionage, including the average soldier. Accordingly the protocols this system is based upon, are designed to be as straightforward as possible, not an adventure in astral travel. These coordinate-based viewing protocols were created to use the viewer's body as a signal processor and to allow the viewer to slowly decode the internal language of the subconscious through the body. In many ways it is a system of sensing rather than viewing because information can come in many different forms. For some people the information tends to be visual, while for others it may be predominantly auditory or tactile.

Viewing Protocols

The viewer begins the viewing process by creating an "ideogram" on paper. The ideogram, a term coined by Ingo Swann, is a graphical representation of the target by the subconscious mind and is done automatically. It serves as a starting place for the viewer. To an outside observer, the ideogram appears as nothing more than a potentially complex, squiggly line on the page. In theory, it allows the subconscious to transfer information in the language of shapes to the conscious mind. These shapes, sometimes referred to as one's own "personal hieroglyphics," are particular to every person; they are the person's unique internal language. To a skilled viewer, the entire description of the target appears encoded within the ideogram. It is a one-dimensional hologram—a window to the etheric.

After drawing their squiggly-looking ideogram, the viewer then probes it with their pen or finger and describes their basic impressions, such as soft, hard, wet, or dry. The ideogram at this point functions like a hologram, allowing the viewer's subconscious to modify the feeling of the person's physical contact with the ink and paper. It may look like a squiggle to an observer, but to the viewer it represents what the physical target might actually feel like if they were to physically touch it. When the viewer has probed their ideogram and described its appearance and feeling, they then make a primitive identification of the basic "gestalt" qualities of the ideogram. Is it manmade, natural, motion/energy, or live-organic? The viewer must at this point pick a basic ideogram descriptor, which describes the basic properties of the target. The point is for the viewer to move into a very basic holistic description without any rational analysis. Analyzing perceptions only serves to activate the left-hemisphere (or logical side) of the brain which interferes with the viewing process.

Ideogram Examples

The following examples show what typical ideograms look like. In each case, the viewer started with nothing more than a blank page. The viewer only receives some coordinate numbers from the session monitor. These numbers are essentially random or the day's date and merely serve to identify to the viewer which folder on the desk in front of him contains the target. These examples also show the viewers' decoding work in phase 1, which is seen in the A:, B:, and C: on the right side of the page. These letters refer to viewers' sense of the motion, feeling, and basic identification of the ideogram.

Figure 3 shows a viewer's ideogram for the target "Launch of Apollo 13 Spacecraft/event (July 16, 1970)." This verbal cue was placed inside a manila folder on a table in front of the viewer. He was given no information beforehand about the cue and simply described his perceptions at they occurred.

Sketch © 2001 by Echan Deravy

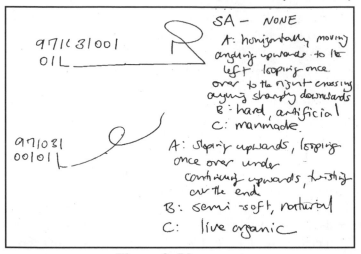

Figure 3: Ideograms

Here the viewer described manmade and live/organics at the target sight. By the end of the session he had described the whole event very well. His post-session summary words were, "Something has happened to a group of beings and an object/structure associated with them. What seemed like a hopeless situation of dazed panic and hot smoky confusion somehow turned around within 48 hours to one of the great breakthroughs by a group of resilient and humorous beings."

Figure 4 shows the ideogram for a target showing a train in a tunnel. The session was done double-blind (a scientific experiment where no specific information is given in advance to any of the parties involved). In this case the viewer produced a multiple ideogram: a line containing the gestalts of three separate aspects of the target all in one. In her identification, she described manmade, air/space, and land as the main elements describing the target.

In her post-session summary she said, "The target has three parts: manmade, air/space, and land. It is smooth/hard, with a grating sound . . . A landmass of rocky dry cold place with whistling sound. A huge orange mass. A luminosity in the background with an inky, dark foreground. The feeling is heavy, dark, other worldly, with a function of industry. A chinking sound."

Sketch © 2001 by Barbara Pals

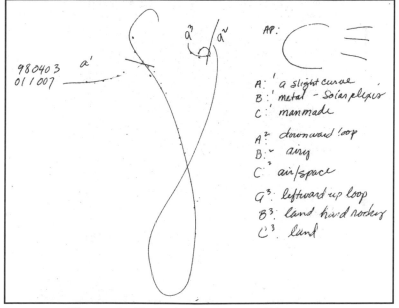

Figure 4: Train in Tunnel and Ideogram

Sketch © 2001 by Lorraine Moller

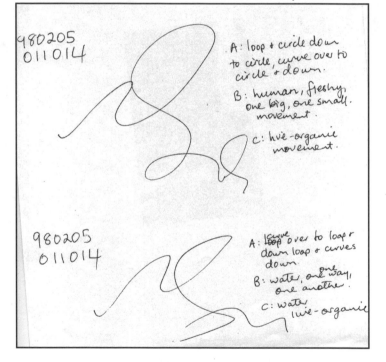

Figure 5: Ideograms for Woman Holding Cat

Figure 5 shows the ideograms for a target of a woman holding a cat. The viewer picked up the gestalts of live/organic and motion/energy. The ideograms are fluid and suggestive of living things. They also appear uninhibited and free-flowing both of which show that the ideogram came from her subconscious mind.

Phases II and III

After Phase I, the viewer can choose to receive a more detailed and in-depth description of the target. In the language of RV, the aperture begins to open and the viewer can perceive more of the target. They will begin to sense more specific information and drawings pertaining to the target. This includes sensory information such as sounds, taste, smells, textures, and ambiance. It can also include dimensional information such as size, direction, patterns, and orientation. This is known as Phases II and III. At some point in describing the target, the viewer will have a physical or emotional reaction to the target, which they write down as a "viewer impression." This viewer impression can often come as a sense of surprise because the viewer's body is reacting to a psychic signal rather than stimuli in their immediate physical surroundings. It is important for the viewer to write down their personal reaction to the target in the form of the viewer impression because it indicates a definitive stage of target contact.

The traditional way to write down Phase II information in CRV is on the left side of the page. The logic of this is that the left side of the page corresponds to the right side of the brain. However, after studying the fractal shapes of Conch shells and galaxies, we decided that a spiral form might also help to elucidate data from the viewer. The idea is that the geometry of the spiral acts like an etheric antenna on the page itself. This spiral form might help the viewer to better tune into the target signal source.

Many objects in nature are built around spirals and this seems to be the shape associated with the movement of energy, such as in the human heart. The spiral is the basis of the Golden Mean or Proportion otherwise known as the Phi-Ratio from Greek science,

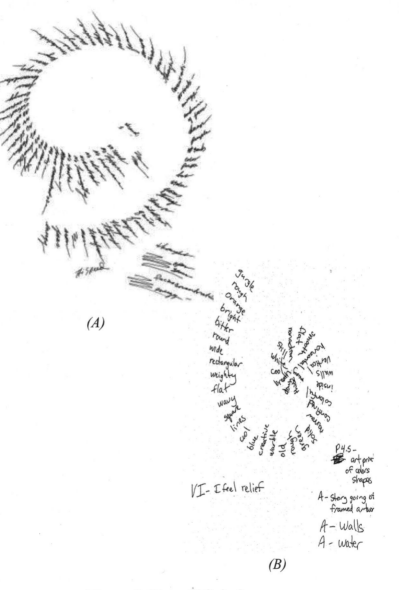

(A)

(B)

Figure 6: Phase II Spirals

which appears throughout the idea of sacred geometry. It also helps to involve the viewer's body to continuously turn the page; many viewers seem to enjoy writing down their data in this fashion.

Subsequent phases include perceptions of higher-order information like concepts, things, and emotions perceived at the target site, in addition to subtle movement exercises to move the viewer around the target in space and time. Viewers can potentially create very detailed drawings of the target and determine complex symbolic relationships between things and people at the site. In general, the viewer moves from more basic information in the beginning phases of the session to more detailed information towards the end.

No matter what stage the viewer is at within the session, the basic principles are the same: to transfer information from the subconscious to the conscious mind with as little coloration and imagination from the conscious mind as possible. The more this process is adhered to, the greater the accuracy of the session. In theory, any thing, person, place, or location can be described in this way. It doesn't matter where it is or when it happened. Tests were done by sending Ingo Swann and Hella Hamid, two SRI viewers, down in a miniature submarine off Los Angeles. These experiments showed that the subspace signal is not electromagnetic; neither water nor distance affected the accuracy as they would a radio signal. The exact nature of the process then is probably outside the realm of normal energy frequencies.

The Directability of Perception

One of the key features of RV is that while it is not produced by mental thought, it can be directed by the viewer's conscious mind. Thus, the viewer can be given verbal cues to move around the target site in space and also in time. The viewer could be instructed, for instance, to move inside a building and walk down the hallways or to move back from the target an appropriate distance to get a more complete perspective. Similarly, viewers can be moved backwards and forwards in time to see how a site or event changes over time. The movements can be very specific down to a few minutes or feet. Apparently, the subconscious mind is very good at locating precise locations and temporal frames and relaying this information between the conscious and viewing minds. These temporal and spacial exercises are relied on heavily in Phase IV of the viewing protocols.

The following photos show initial targets and viewers' accurate descriptions. In each case, the target was randomly selected from a large pool of over 100 possible pictures. Each session had a monitor who saw the target in advance. However, the monitor gave no information to the viewer about their pre-selected targets. I was present at each of these sessions.

Figure 7 shows a photo of the Washington Monument and the viewer's drawing. In this session, the viewer actually saw the monument in his mind's eye and then mentally walked down the nearby reflecting pool. He then described the Lincoln Memorial, which is just opposite the Washington Monument.

The viewer in Figure 8 drew the shape of the race car very accurately. He then started to fill in the stadium, but began to doubt himself. In his mind he thought, "This cannot be a car in a stadium." Unsure of his data, he ended the session before filling in any more information despite its accuracy.

*Washington
Monument*

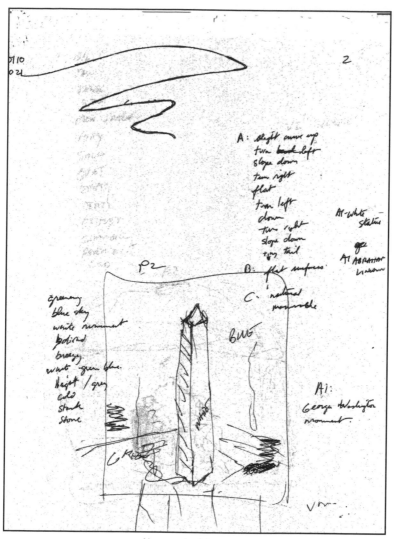

Viewer's Drawing

Sketch © 1998 by Wells Christie

Figure 7: Washington Monument and Sketch

Sketch © 1997 by Ron Russell

Race Car

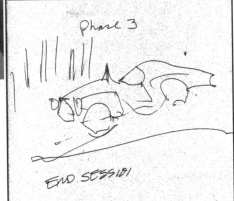

Viewer's Drawing

Figure 8: Race Car and Sketch

Very often when viewers get accurate information, they begin to question their data and may edit out the most precise information they are sensing. Some believe that this occurs because the conscious mind does not want to give up its control of the flow of information to the subconscious mind. Thus, it throws out the baby with the bath water. With proper training, the viewer's conscious mind learns to enjoy the viewing process and will, in time, aid in the viewing process. Initially, viewers may feel some resistance to letting go of their typical mental habits, such as feeling in control of one's body and perceptions.

The target in Figure 9, a Saturn V liftoff, was viewed several years later by the same viewer who viewed the racecar. Here he was able to draw the target as well as write the following post-session summary, "I see a desert, like an aircraft/rocket proving ground, some people are thrilled, fire from rocket or craft in air, smoke and some danger."

(A) Rocket Picture

Sketch © 1999 by Ron Russell

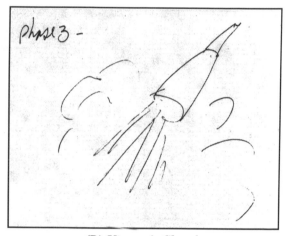

(B) Viewer's Sketch

Figure 9: Rocket Sketch

Figure 10 shows a target photo of a Greek Harbor, with a close-up photo of the ship in the middle-left section of the picture. In this case, the viewer was able to accurately reproduce the ship. His post-session summary reads, "Man-made object(s), looks like ship or vessel or barge passing in front of harbor with city (town) in background, cloudy (partly cloudy) day with breeze (cool breeze), salty feeling."

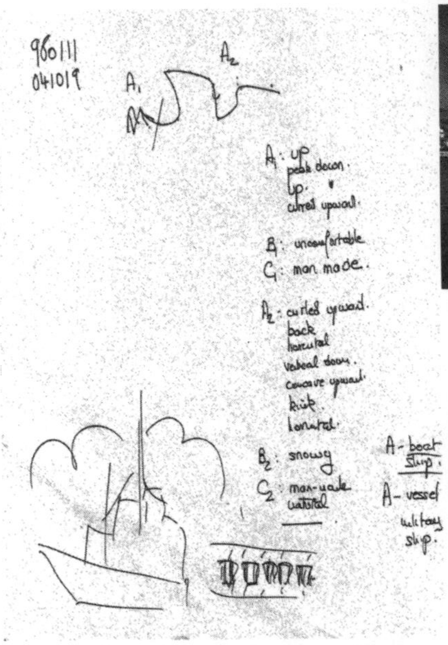

(B) Greek Harbor

(A)   Viewer's Drawing

(C) Closeup

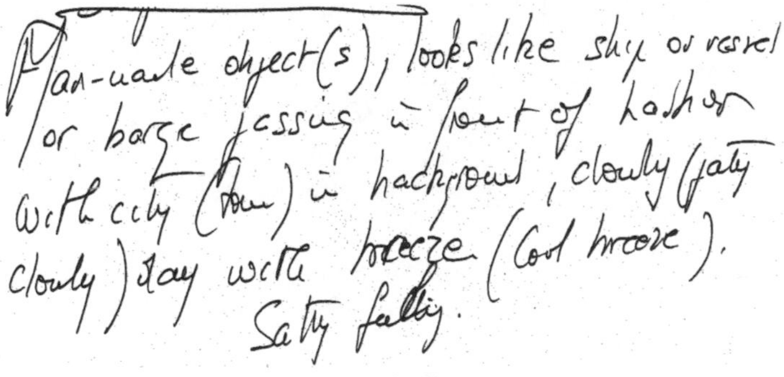

(D) Viewer's Summary

Sketch and Summary © 2001 by Bernard Amadei

Figure 10: Harbor Scene and Session

Figure 11 is an example of a double-blind session where neither the viewer, monitor, nor anyone else in the room knew the target's identity in advance. Nonetheless, the viewer was able to describe the target accurately. She drew some good sketches of the picture. Her Phase IV information also shows good target contact. Her session summary read,: "Sea, sky, beach, storm? Choppy, someone in trouble, boat? Someone watching, wants to help, howling, scaring, black, blue, white, capsizing and wooden boat?"

(A) Boat

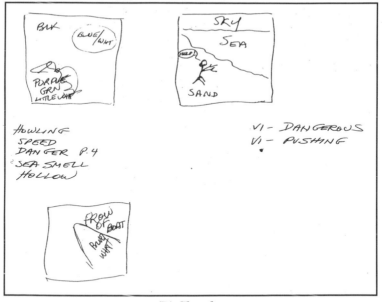

(B) Sketches

(C) Viewer's Summary

Sketch and Summary © 2001 by Frances Lewis

Figure 11: Boat, Sketch, and Summary

Figure 12 is also an example of a double-blind session. In this case, the viewer focused exclusively on the drawing of the juggler and ignored the main picture, in this case a computer. This is known as "door-knobbing," an effect whereby the viewer views the doorknob, so to speak, but not the door itself. Movement exercises, often given by the session monitor, can be used to move the viewer around the target area in time and space. This allows the viewer to obtain as much information as possible.

(A) Target Photo   Sketch © 2001 by Lorraine Moller

(B) Viewer's Sketch

Figure 12: Computer Person and Sketch

Advanced Sessions

After a viewer has acquired basic viewing skills and has a good track record against verifiable, known targets, it is often challenging for them to view more enigmatic targets. This can include things like crop circles, extraterrestrials and UFOs. Figure 13 shows the Milk Hill formation of 1997 and one viewer's description.

In this summary, the viewer described the purpose of the target was to "break contact with the real world." The target site "seems to be a fun place to be—forget about your cares—fast, fun, frivolous—gives the feeling of freedom—escape, openness—

outdoors . . . Sun, warmth, hot, has a cool open feeling too—roaring sounds, rumbling—shaking—fast movement, lots of white powerful energy—viewer impression of an avalanche—I know there is something massive in the picture which is a focal point—that has much energy, fast moving yet stationary - like a roller coaster . . .."

Interestingly, there were roaring sounds heard in nearby Alton Barnes the night the formation in question appeared.

Two weeks after completing this session the viewer was driving near her home in Estes Park, Colorado, when she saw a glowing green ball the size of a compact automobile streaking across the mountains. Moving at a fast speed, the ball then stopped two blocks in front of her car as she approached a stop sign. She could tell from her dashboard clock that the object stayed motionless for two minutes. Just as suddenly as it appeared, it sped off again and stopped a few blocks down the road, then raced off over the horizon. It should also be pointed out that this viewer had no interest in UFOs or crop circles before doing this session.

(A) Milk Hill Formation
Photo © 1997 Ron Russell

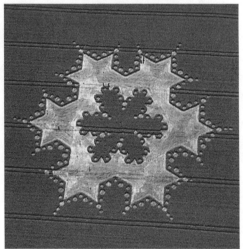

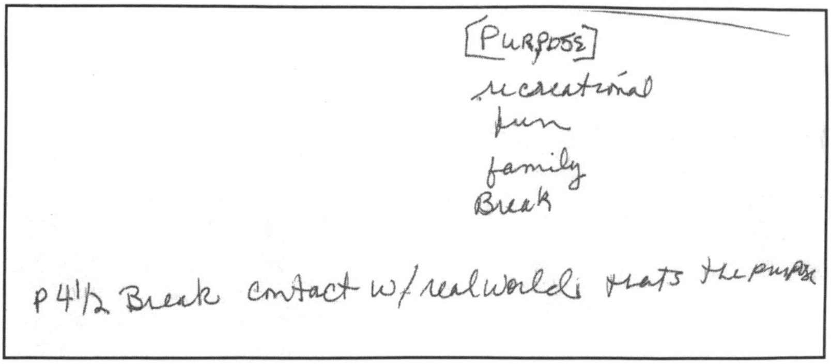

(B) Viewer Description

Session data © 2001 by Mary Darracott
Figure 13: Milk Hill Formation and Viewer's Description

Other types of esoteric targets I have participated in include the Galactic Federation Headquarters, which is apparently the bureaucratic administrative center of our particular area of the galaxy. This target often appears as a shiny metal building in the middle of a desert-like planet.

Another frequently viewed target is the Martian colony under Mount Baldy near Santa Fe, New Mexico. These extraterrestrials were apparently first viewed by some of the military viewers. Viewers describe this area as a forested, mountain environment with networks of tunnels below. These tunnels contain humanoid-like beings working in small groups with advanced technologies.

With regard to verification, we cannot know for sure what the viewers are perceiving. However, we can say that their results are consistent and may be accurate. Perhaps the future will contain the appropriate feedback for these targets.

Verbal Cues

Targets do not need to be pictures; they can also be of verbal cues written on a piece of paper and then hidden. The viewer's subconscious picks up on the intent of the cue and receives the appropriate information. For example in an intermediate class the viewer was given the target cue, "Wright Brothers/1st Manned Flight/Kitty Hawk/" as a group of events. The viewer did her session and wrote down the following summary:

> "The target contains something manmade and natural. There is an activity like an exhibition. The activity involves some kind of movement, like floating/ flying. If I did it, I would feel, comfortable, light. The movement is forward and has expansion. People are watching it. They are impressed by the activity."

In some cases viewers are able to accurately read words from the target. In the military's protocols this was known as Stage 7, a final stage in a viewing session where the viewer attempts to write letters and pronounce words associated with the target. Sometimes, however, this occurs spontaneously at any stage in the session. In one instance, we gave a viewer a target with a basket of food and the caption above read, "How many miles did you get today?" The viewer wrote in her session summary: "A bountiful plenty, as if one would go *miles* for it in order to be fed."

What seems to be important in verbal cues is the intent the writer wants to portray in the cue. This intent becomes embedded in the words they choose and their feelings when putting them on the page. The viewer spontaneously detects this intent and may reproduce some or all of the words perfectly without any previous clue or hint about the target.

Viewing the Future: Zero-Point Energy Devices

Zero-point energy machines are devices that theoretically tap into the vacuum of space and transfer energy into our physical reality. While there are presently no commercially available machines like this, there are many working models that various inventors say could someday eliminate the need for fossil fuels and other deleterious forms of energy generation. Starting in 1998, we began to view some of the potential devices in the near future that could perform such a task. We have thought of it as a form of technology transfer from the future. The target cue would typically read something like, "Most likely zero-point energy device used on Earth in near future."

One such device was a cone-shaped structure that seemed to involve the use of colloidal metals suspended in liquid-filled coils that rotated around a metallic core. Apparently the device reverses the flow of entropy by creating coherent heat transfer. Some viewers detected a semi-sentient membrane surrounding the device. Some of the materials were mined from the Earth, but the membrane seemed to be made of polymer gels. In our viewing sessions we perceived that this device would be in use within ten to twenty years on Earth. It would be housed in a medium-sized box located in peoples' backyards and would generate electricity. Cars or hovercraft, for that matter, could house smaller versions. It is interesting to note that when some magazines in the Fall of 2000 wrote news articles about fuel-cell technologies that create electricity from hydrogen and oxygen, they mentioned the use of a "proton exchange membrane" as a center-piece of the technology. Perhaps our sessions were on the mark—only time will tell.

Figure 14 contains a viewer's drawing of this cone-shaped zero-point energy device. It stands a few feet high and is entirely designed around Phi-Ratio (golden mean) geometry. The spiral in the middle represents a colloidal solution moving through tubing placed around a metallic core.

The Answer is in Your Body

One thing certain about the RV process is that it accesses the viewer's autonomic nervous system. Meaning once the viewer is locked onto the target, their body seems to go into autopilot. The viewer may not even comprehend what they are doing, but the information can be just as accurate regardless. The decoding process is centered around interpreting the body's communications through the autonomic nervous system. The process is subconscious in the sense that, just like heart and breathing activity, the viewer does not need to consciously know what is going on for the system to work perfectly. If one thinks about the trillions of interactions relating to respiration, transformation, immune system function, and elimination that occur in our bodies each second, it is truly an awesome process—the conscious mind does not need to be involved at all.

Sketch © 2001 by Author

**Figure 14: Zero-Point Energy Device
Detected in Viewing Sessions**

The main principle of Stanford's RV protocols is to reduce the noise of the conscious mind relative to the strength of the psychic signal. While the noise of the mental mind can be very loud, the psychic signal tends to be very fleeting and transient. The viewer must act like a detective continually weeding out the noise from the true signal. As most of us in the West have been conditioned to think our way through problems and mind puzzles, there is a tendency for us to try to guess what the target is. The guesses are usually (though not always) inaccurate. The conscious mind is used to getting information from the five senses; when these signals are dimmed, the logical brain is unusually ineffective in solving the problem of acquiring accurate target descriptors. However, some of the conscious guesswork may be *close* to the mark, and a shrewd viewer can sometimes use analytical noise to hone in on the actual target.

The main principle of the protocols is to write every thought down and not edit anything at all. Verb and adjective descriptors, what are termed "low-level thoughts," tend to be more accurate when compared to "high-level thoughts" like specific nouns and concepts. These latter definitions are initially written down on the right margin of the page and deemed by the viewer as "analytical overlay." The overlay is acknowledged and then released. In contrast, the descriptive verbs and adjectives are kept on the left and middle of the page as data.

The reasoning for this process is that the left-brain controls the right side of our body and vice versa. The left-brain is also responsible for sequential and linear thought. In Betty Edward's book, *Drawing on the Right Side of the Brain*, she puts forth the idea that holistic, image-based thinking is the province of the right hemisphere of the brain. This is borne out by our experience with RV, which seems to rely on the right side of the brain. The psychic signal appears to be connected to the right side of the brain more than the left. The essential point is that our logical and analytical approach to things limits and reduces the overall information flow in our minds. Switching to non-analytical perception seems to enhance psychic information flow by increasing our mental bandwidth. The RV process switches the viewer out of the logical mode, and into a free-flowing thought mode. In doing so, the viewer can access new frequencies of information.

Chaos Theory in Action

The experience of doing an RV session can feel very confusing to the viewer precisely because they must relinquish logical control over the data flow. The conscious mind ceases to act like a filter and takes on a role like that of an orchestra conductor, coordinating the action of all the players. Paradoxically, a general rule of thumb is that the more confusing the session data is to the viewer, the more accurate it is likely to be. Because the data acquisition process is non-linear with the subconscious mind "winking" around the target site, it can grab pieces of information in a noncontiguous way. In general, the viewer is given nothing more than a blank sheet of paper; thus the conscious mind has nothing to base results on and, in theory, gives up control to the subconscious. The data begins to flow, but it appears to be a random stream of words and images with no obvious coherency. At this point the viewer can feel very confused.

However, if she is willing to tolerate this confusion for a few moments, her mind will engage in a process of self-organization, and the data will gradually achieve some degree of coherency. The data flows at a faster rate and begins to gain a semblance of internal order. The viewer may not have a clue as to what he is describing, but the data stream may begin to possess the hallmarks of some internal consistency. Towards the end of the session, if the viewer is on target, the images and impressions of the target may grow stronger in magnitude. At this point the viewer may cease to feel confused and may just go along with the flow of the data which is quite accurate.

It appears the viewer's mind is taking its cues from a nonphysical source of information. Voluntarily detached from the body's sense organs, the mind then seeks its information flow from an etheric source of frequencies, which are readily available to us. We typically don't rely on these frequencies in a conscious, waking state. When the conscious mind is out of the way, these frequencies become more transparent and accessible, allowing the viewer to hone in on the information. If the process works properly, the viewer completes this transition from physical to nonphysical in the beginning of the session and then spends the rest of her time decoding this etheric information. In essence, the viewer's mind moves from order to chaos and then back to order at a higher frequency than before.

5. **Discovering the Alien Within:**
Subspace Travels at Farsight

Balls Of Light at Farsight

THE PROCESS OF USING ETHERIC frequencies to describe a non-local target involves energies and phenomena that we do not yet understand. Nearly everyone who has been involved with RV has had some experience with what may be called, for lack of a better word, the paranormal. Skeptics may say this has to do with the mental instability inherent to the RV process. However, some of these experiences have multiple witnesses, such as those at SRI which are described by author Jim Schnabel. Some of the original researchers, when they began experimenting with RV, experienced UFO's floating in their homes, strange animals in their houses, and in the case of Targ and Putoff, the appearance of a robotic type of human who pounded on their hotel room door until they let him in. He walked around as if blind and then promptly left.

My first contact with this type of weird, non-ordinary phenomena had to do with balls of light at the Farsight Institute during an RV session in 1997. The viewer was a student in training—let's call him Bob, a transportation expert from the Southwest. As was often the case towards the end of a Farsight training course, Bob had been given an extraterrestrial target, "Martian Bureaucratic-Technical Elite (current time)". In theory, this cue should have put Bob's subconscious in contact with the closest possible representation of Martian scientists and engineers in the current time. One could design any sort of cue imaginable using this format. Historical targets are also possible, and the data are easier to verify at the end of the session.

In this case, Bob started his session "blind" (with no conscious knowledge of the target). His session took place in North Atlanta in a room at the multi-leveled Holiday Inn where the classes were held. After about one half-hour into the session, he felt as though someone was touching him on the shoulder. He thought it was his monitor, Lucy, but she had been sitting in a chair across the room the entire time. The feeling of the presence behind him left him feeling strange, so he told Lucy he was going to take a break and leave the room for a few moments.

According to Bob, he went out on the porch to get some air and then came in and started the session again. As Bob was sitting at the desk, a ball of light, about the size of a large beach ball, appeared right over Bob's desk, about two feet in front of him. In a state of amazement, Bob just stared at it for a few moments. He described it to me later as looking like a clear, glassy Christmas tree ornament with something sparkling and glowing in the center. He wanted to touch it and gradually moved his hands towards it. He put his fingertips on the ball, felt the upper surface, and started to move his hands downward to the 3 and 9 o'clock positions. As he did, he received a sharp, burning shock in his hands. Lucy heard him scream but did not see the ball. Bob told me it felt like dipping his hands into molten lead—it was the most painful thing he had ever experienced. Then suddenly his mind was filled with ideas regarding his target. The next thing he wrote was, "Energy and Guidance in a magnitude of Galactic proportions, rescue . . ." He continued to write about one full page of information about Greys and Martians. From that moment on, his session seemed extremely accurate. Bob was upset about the whole affair, but later felt as though the ball of light had been there to help him with his RV session.

Extraterrestrial Viewing Targets

By conventional standards (if there are such things in the world of RV), Farsight targets were often way out there. The target could be anything from an historical event, an astronomical target, or ETs and otherworldly spirits. Courtney believed that RV was best used as an educational tool for familiarizing people with the unknown. As he put it, the Farsight Institute was a "fear reduction program" allowing people to overcome their superstitions and age-old beliefs about the "dark forces" that are so prevalent in some cultures. For this reason, we were often tasked with targets that presented totally new ideas and energies to us.

For myself, viewing ETs and crop circles certainly took the cake in terms of novelty, though historical targets and plain-old calibration targets were just as challenging. In many ways, it felt liberating to be able to sense what was happening at the Face on Mars thousands of years ago or on Earth in the future. While there was no way to verify this type of "esoteric" information, we could cross-check our sessions with each other to see if there was some consistency across all the sessions done by the group at that time. And even that type of analysis raised the question of whether we were all just generating a collective "storyline" as Courtney called it. Russell Targ later told me that group sessions have the potential to create telepathic overlay from one individual to the next. Therefore at the Stanford Research Institute, the researchers always preferred one session at a time. Nonetheless, this telepathic overlay seemed to be genuinely true and had its own life well beyond the length of a session. In many ways, it seemed to determine the course of the whole institute.

At Farsight, rumors would often circulate that "so and so" was an ally of the "bad" ETs or some such gossip, or that the person did not believe in the existence of a certain type of ETs. In the end, such talk was inevitably destructive to the morale of the group. This group gossip was unverifiable and though tempting to engage in, seemed to make a weird experience even weirder.

The connection between remote viewing and non-human life forms is not new: the Stanford group and the military viewers at Fort Meade also had their experience with viewing extraterrestrials. While none of this type of viewing was officially tasked by the U.S. Government, it was not discouraged either. At the First Annual CRV Conference, 1999, in Mescalero, New Mexico, former

Lieutenant "Skip" Atwater presented information about Pat Price's ET viewing sessions at SRI. According to everyone who knew him, Pat was one of the most accurate viewers anyone had ever known. A former police chief in Burbank, California, Price had informally used his viewing skills to apprehend criminals in his jurisdiction. He had come into SRI by responding to a newspaper ad they had placed in a local paper. If Pat viewed it, "You could take it to the bank" as one retired military viewer told me.

Skip recollected how one day Price had come into SRI with viewings and sketches of four extraterrestrial bases on Earth. According to Price, these were located in Alaska, Spain, Australia, and Zimbabwe. Each base had a specific function and was concealed under a mountain. Price was deeply fearful of these entities and felt they were covertly infiltrating and subverting our society. Skip reiterated that Price had done these viewings on his own, unasked. Sometime later, however, viewers Joe McMoneagle and Mel Riley were given these targets, one of them double-blind, and they came up with similar results.

Recently, Ingo Swann published the book *Penetration* (1998) that detailed his work for a secret organization within the federal government. He had spent about one week in the 1970s at an ultra-secret underground base outside of Washington, D.C., viewing the moon and mysterious activities going on there. He claimed to have been in contact with this organization for an extended period of time while he worked at SRI. They even took him to Alaska once to see a triangular-shaped UFO sucking water out of a lake; apparently these people wanted him to view the craft and find out what it was doing there. According to Swann, this secret governmental organization was deeply concerned about the extraterrestrial presence on Earth and the Moon to the extent that they were even concerned about his own safety after his viewing sessions. Apparently there was some feeling that the lunar extraterrestrials had telepathic abilities of their own and were not friendly to humans. Hal Puthoff, who directed SRI with Russell Targ at the time, says about Swann's claims, that "Ingo didn't make it up." Therefore, between Swann and Price's ET viewing work, it seems clear that extraterrestrials have been linked to human viewing activities since the beginning of the modern remote-viewing era.

One of the targets that we frequently viewed at Farsight was a Martian Underground Base under Mount Baldy just north of Santa Fe, New Mexico. Courtney had originally viewed this target while working with his trainer and was convinced that the results of his session were accurate: that extraterrestrials, in this case Martians, were living under Mount Baldy. Courtney gave this target to his Farsight viewers fairly often and many of us came up with the same type of data. This included extraterrestrials, advanced technology, and cramped underground living quarters. The story seemed to be that these beings had come here from Mars to escape environmental catastrophe millions of years ago in their time. They had been brought forward in time by the Greys to live on Earth. Sometime in the near future they would make themselves known to humans.

Once I established the Mount Baldy Institute in Boulder, we continued to view the same target with the same results. Viewers would often pick up on the pine forests and the mountain itself, then the beings living under the mountain and their novel technological systems. Whether this was merely a continuing storyline or accurate data will only be known in the future. I can say that the viewing data on this target tends to be fairly consistent from year to year so the viewers are probably picking up on something real.

One of the more esoteric sessions I did was on a target called the "Grey's Interdimensional Gateway Near Earth." This is, apparently, a portal of sorts that these ETs use to get into our solar system from wherever they are. Of course, while there is no way to verify this type of target data, it was an enjoyable experience as the perceptions I had during the session were far from ordinary. Figure 15 below is a drawing from the session.

Drawing © 2001 by Author

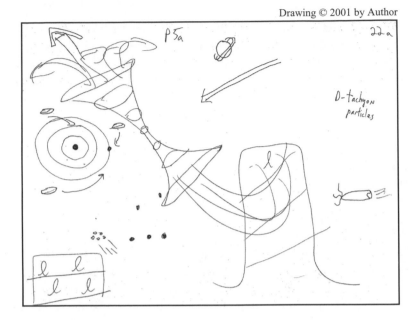

Figure 15: Grey's Gateway Dimension Near Earth

Lizard People and Sex with Extraterrestrials

Bob, the Farsight viewer mentioned earlier, continued to have weird experiences with RV that went beyond the manifestation of strange phenomena during viewing sessions. Several months later he had more disturbing encounters. First was the feeling of having been contacted by a huge, lizard-like human as he was dozing off to sleep. He was taking a nap in the late afternoon when the vision of a seven-foot, orange-skinned humanoid appeared in his mind. He clearly remembered it turning towards him from a distance of about ten feet and making eye contact. Bob felt frightened and then popped out of his daydreaming state. I would have believed that this was all in Bob's imagination except that his description was similar to other people's experiences. In fact, the monitor of his Martian session, where he encountered the ball of light over his desk, called him out of the blue several days after his encounter with the Lizard. Immediately he knew why she had called and told her about the

Lizard encounter. Lucy was dumbfounded because she had a similar experience a few days prior and that was precisely why she was calling him.

Bob's next experience was even more disconcerting. Before going on, I should mention that Bob is the type of person whom anyone would find credible, honest, and straightforward. There is no doubt in my mind that he believed to be true what he told me about the following incident. Though he gave me some information about it over the phone, he wouldn't give me any details and insisted that I come down to Tucson to meet him. Several months later I drove down to visit a friend who had also taken the Farsight classes and was a friend of Bob's as well. We all met over breakfast and he told me this story. He then gave me a written version of his account; looking it over, it read like a pornographic novel.

Bob told me that on the day of this encounter, he was scheduled to make a night trip. During the afternoon he listened to some Hemisync tapes from the Monroe Institute and then decided to nap for a few hours. It was exactly 2:00 p.m. as he put his head on the pillow. As he reached back to grab the pillow, with his head still facing forward, he suddenly saw a naked woman at the foot of the bed:

> Her facial features were very fine, a slender nose, thin lips, ears that were perfectly formed and in proportion. Her hair was a light straw blond, slightly more than shoulder length swept back, not a look of being well- kept, but a healthy, not thin type, and pleasant to look at. There was no body smell or smell of breath. There was no odor at all.

His first reaction on seeing her was that she clearly was not human. Her characteristics included medium height with slightly grayish-looking skin. She had small breasts and genitals but no pubic hair. He immediately asked her what she was doing in his room. Telepathically she told him that she was from an extraterrestrial race called the Greys and that they had been attempting to increase their reproductive ability. They had, in the past, lost their ability to breed naturally and had only recently regained their fertility. While their males had the ability to copulate, they didn't have the inclination to do so. So females like herself were seeking out human partners. She said she was a virgin and desired to have sex with Bob right there on the spot. Bob said that he was married and that it would be morally wrong to have sexual intercourse with her. Apparently, the being didn't agree with him and shortly thereafter he felt paralyzed.

The female Grey then proceeded to position herself on top of him and began rubbing her genitals over him. She would arch her back and move her breasts back and forth on top of him. The opening of her vagina was small, but she was able to insert Bob's penis partly inside of her. At one point, she telepathically transmitted an image to Bob of her hymen to show him that it was unbroken. Bob said to her several times that he would prefer oral sex to intercourse but she wasn't interested:

As she heightened in her emotions, she also tightened her hold (grip) on my mind, she was controlling totally all of my body, my response to her actions upon me, my erection, my body responded in ways that are not to be described.

There was never a feeling of an orgasm, the sensation of what she was doing to me physically and mentally, the control of my physical mind, somewhere early on I was taken past that plateau without realizing it.

To understand sexually where I was taken is not in my ability to describe it in totality. Think of leaving earth, looking back and seeing the sun as a pinpoint of light! I fall short in this description also.

As her actions increased, more penetration was allowed with increased rotation of her hips, only it increased very slowly. This action seemed endless, time was slowing down for me. I think it was the grasp she had on my mind which tightened as penetration increased . . . At or near the end, I lost all feeling physically, all went blank.

She seemed to climax several times and Bob remembers getting groggier until he was almost asleep. All of sudden he regained movement of his body:

> My next feeling, a snap back, a jolt, a feeling of fright, a feeling of uncertainty of where I was. I leaped from my bed, in one step I bounced backwards against a wall five feet away. I was looking back at my bed. She was gone, I was back to full reality but possibly the hardest to handle mentally was yet to come.

He looked down at his penis to see if this had all been a daydream and to his horror found that his penis was greatly disfigured. His now flaccid penis was 10 to 12 inches long. It hung down to his knees and was the thickness of a person's wrist. Upon seeing this he collapsed onto the rug of his bedroom in shock. He then dragged himself to the bathroom and placed his penis over the rim of the toilet. At that point he had an orgasm and ejaculated. According to Bob, it took about six hours for his penis to regain its normal shape and size.

As can be expected, Bob was upset by this incident and felt that his body had been violated. If it weren't for his rock-solid character and worldly experience, I would have thought it too inconceivable to be true. But knowing Bob, I choose to believe him. It is also important to point out that other people have experienced similar incidents including a tribal chief in Africa who reported his story to John Mack, a psychologist and "abduction" researcher at Harvard University.

Ron Russell, of Denver, Colorado (who has taken several of the crop circle photos in this book) had a similar experience. Though this occurred to him in a dream state, it had repercussions the next day in his waking life. He remembers that in his dream he was sitting on a bed in a bedroom with his friend, Shari, who was sitting on a couch about thirty feet away. Then a small, female humanoid being with big, dark glasses appeared at the side of the bed, got in next to him, spoke to him telepathically, and initiated intimacy. Ron noticed she had no genitals and her breasts were higher than on a human. Nonetheless, she became very orgasmic and turned into light in his arms. Ron then experienced an ecstatic, blissful feeling.

The next day, Ron met Shari at another location. Shari was angry and Ron asked her what was wrong. She said she had a dream the night before where she was sitting on a couch and Ron was in a nearby bed. Then a "little hussy," as Shari put it, appeared in the bedroom. Shari remembered seeing Ron making love with the humanoid without inviting Shari to join in and this upset her. She was astonished when Ron told her details of the dream.

Interestingly, Philip Krapf, the former metro desk editor for the *L.A. Times*, in his book *The Contact has Begun* (1998), describes being taken aboard an extraterrestrial ship and having one of the female beings there suggest that they have sex. Krapf remembers she had no pubic hair, and her breasts were also slightly higher than on a human, a feature that turned him off somewhat. He was also married.

It isn't clear exactly what is going on here, given that some of these accounts happened in dream-time and others did not. But the parallels between these various accounts are quite intriguing.

Close Encounters

One of the persistent ideas at Farsight was that those of us who were there were all, periodically, being detained or abducted, depending on your point of view, at night on spaceships operated by Greys: a short, large-eyed species with gray skin, apparently from the star system Zeta Reticuli. Almost every one of the instructors at Farsight had this experience at one time or another. It was hard to say whether this was just some sort of sociological phenomenon, the effect of being in a group together in strange circumstances for a week or two at a time, or whether it was "really" physically happening. But it probably didn't matter, for as long as people talked about and planned for it, the phenomena became real enough.

In January of 1997, I had my own experience with this phenomenon. I awoke at about 4:30 a.m. in my hotel room which was located on the second floor. All was quiet so I went back to sleep. What I remember next was the impression that I was flying in a small, circular automobile with three smaller, slightly-built, bald humanoids sitting beside and behind me. The beings reminded me of kindergarten friends I hadn't seen in thrity years. The vehicle we were in pitched forward and back, and the surroundings were completely dark. The next thing I knew, I was in a large, circular, dome-shaped room with lots of tables. My companions were nowhere to be seen. One larger person, behind a bar-like desk at the front of the room, appeared to be in charge. He seemed to be a bartender. I approached him and he offered me clear liquid in a glass, saying it would make me feel better. The next thing I knew I was led to one of the metal tables. I lay down on it and soon felt paralyzed. It was an uncomfortable feeling, and I was upset about the situation. I lay there for what felt like two hours, then suddenly found I could move again. I got up and walked to the "bartender." He said I was free to go. I pointed out to him that I had no money or clothing, and he calmly said all these things would be there when I got home. I remember wanting to call the police, but after another quick trip in the auto-like vehicle, I found myself in my bed staring at the TV across the room. My wallet and keys were right on top of the TV.

I felt completely exhausted as if I had a hangover and it lasted for the next eight hours. I was a wreck. Someone even came up to me and asked what was wrong. She said my eyes appeared to be vibrating back and forth. Whatever had happened left physiological consequences like none I had ever experienced before, effects that were even perceivable to others.

Two nights later I had a dream where I was being shown new remote viewing protocols. They involved using more of the body, such as both hands at once, to acquire viewing data. I told this to Courtney, who asked me to write down my experience. He told me he had been expecting me to receive new protocols; these dream-learned methods later became part of Farsight's advanced protocols known as the "Subspace Probe." When I explained to him how uncomfortable it was to lie paralyzed on a metal table, he suggested

I look at it from the Greys' point of view. They had come all the way from god knows where, taken me out of my bed to somewhere else, and then returned me all in one piece.

Courtney had earlier learned from Prudence's "little Grey dude" that I would be receiving these new viewing methods. Prudence Calabrese originally worked at the Institute as the web designer and went on to become a very accurate viewer and instructor in her own right (see www.LargerUniverse.com). Ever since she began working at Farsight, Prudence received nightly communications from a Grey being that showed up in a hallway outside of her bedroom. This being would inform her of important issues facing the Farsight Institute, sort of like a private intelligence service. Courtney would get these reports in the morning and take appropriate measures.

About one week after I left the Farsight Institute, strange things began to happen in my bedroom at night. One time I woke up to see this blue, semi-solid ball of light moving around my room. I closed my eyes, thinking I was making it up. Opening my eyes again, I still saw the ball up towards the ceiling. After a few seconds, it vanished.

A few days later, I was wakened at close to five in the morning by a voice talking very loudly in my ear. I didn't open my eyes all the way but, was awake enough to realize where I was. The voice sounded as if a person was standing right next to me. The voice began to tell me how it might be a good idea to start a remote viewing center in Boulder, where I was living. It was explained to me that this area was some sort of central node in the region, and the world would benefit from more remote viewing education. The voice was very direct and to the point—there was no joking around. The voice told me that it was one of three entities assigned to look after me. I could see the other two entities hovering nearby. The first entity informed me that if I set up an RV teaching center, people would come to it. I wanted to ask more questions, but even before I could phrase my sentences, the entities were gone—leaving behind the sound of empty wind. I then woke up, and felt the most exhilarating sensation I have ever experienced. It was a combination of joy, self-confidence, power, and abandonment. I felt as if I were flying over the Earth. About ten days later I found an office space for the Mount Baldy Institute and began setting up my research center in Boulder.

Evaluating the Farsight Viewing Experience

The Farsight Institute introduced many of us to the idea of ETs and the possibility of interacting with humanoid life forms in ways we never before considered. Viewing Martians on Mars from millions of years ago or the Grey home world at its zenith were certainly new experiences for most of us. It has to be kept in mind that even though many of these sessions produced consistent and similar types of data across many different viewing sessions, there is no way at the present time to get feedback on these types of "exotic" targets. As accurate feedback is generally essential to one's overall viewing experience, these types of non-ordinary targets need to be evaluated as unknowns, given the lack of solid feedback. Viewing the Eiffel Tower is different from viewing the Face on Mars, as plenty of humans go to the former and none, to our knowledge, have yet visited the latter.

Having said that, it should be recognized that many of the Farsight viewers I knew had very accurate track records when it came to verifiable targets. It makes sense to suppose that because they were accurate on known targets, they should most likely be accurate on all types of targets. But there is no way to know for sure. In any case, these types of non-ordinary and non-verifiable targets introduced us to new possibilities and the potential for interaction with the larger universe. In that sense, whether they could be verified or not, the ET targets served an important function of introducing us to previously unknown life forms and non-discussed topics. At the very least, we seriously considered the idea of interacting with extraterrestrials and that, in itself, had important ramifications. Whether the sessions themselves were fact or fiction remains to be seen.

The Hale-Bopp Incident

In October of 1996, startling news hit the airwaves that an object had been sighted in the vicinity of the approaching comet Hale-Bopp. An amateur astronomer in Texas, Chuck Sramek, claimed to have filmed a large object next to the comet. Excitement grew as some speculated this might be an extraterrestrial craft. To many of us, this seemed to like the perfect opportunity to show the world the value of remote viewing. Courtney had secretly received some photographs from an observatory in Hawaii that purportedly showed the same object next to the comet. These photos, which were later shown to have been falsified, were seen by us as smoking gun evidence. We were even led to believe that the "astronomer" who took the Hawaii photos was going to hold a press conference announcing the discovery of the object. As it turned out, the Farsight Institute had been set up.

On the night when Courtney was scheduled to be on the Art Bell radio show with its 20 million listeners around the world, he commissioned three sessions to be done on the object so he would have something specific to say on the show. It seemed like the perfect opportunity to use RV in a beneficial and publicly interesting way. I received a call from Courtney's assistant, Dale, on that night at around 8:00 p.m. requesting that myself and a visiting friend who had also attended Farsight do a session on the object.

I ended up being the monitor/observer for the session, and my friend Linda, after some persuasion, did the viewing. We did the session, and Linda ended up getting a lot of information about comets and NASA's inability to study this particular one correctly. Other viewers that night got roughly similar results drawings pictures of comets and other general space objects. Linda did include some mental noise about extraterrestrials in her session but did not include these perceptions in her data. Her session was mainly about outer space and a misidentified object in the sky.

Nonetheless, when Courtney got on Art Bell's radio show, he read the session to Art including the mental noise concerning ETs. Thus, in my opinion, he failed to separate out the viewers' signals about comets from their general mental noise about space and the universe. We ended up misinterpreting the data from these sessions and gave everyone listening to the show the startling conclusion that an inhabited object four times the size of the earth was trailing Hale-Bopp. In essence, the ETs were making a fantastic trip past Earth. As Courtney said that night "Art, when the ETs do something, they do it in a big way."

Unfortunately, we had read into the viewing sessions what we wanted to see there. Coupled with the phony photos, we were misled by our own lack of discernment. There simply was no object following Hale-Bopp. The viewing sessions had been explorations of the idea of the comet itself. It took some of us several months to figure out and learn the importance of accurate data interpretation. The Farsight Institute suffered in the eyes of public opinion for this error, though it was a good experience to learn how to interpret data without the color of one's own prejudice.

Interdimensional Channeling

How we learned the truth about the Hale-Bopp incident is a story in itself. Back at the Farsight Institute in the late spring of 1996, I met a man from Los Angeles who told me about a channeled entity named "Bashar" who had talked about Courtney's book, *Cosmic Voyage* (1996), even before it had been published. Channeling is a state of mind in which a person, generally voluntarily, would translate the thoughts of a distant person or entity directly into their native language. In doing so, the channelled would act as a mouth piece for the other intelligence and translate their thoughts in real time, either consciously or in a trance state. In this case, the channeller was Daryl Anka, the brother of singer Paul Anka, and the entity being channeled was apparently an extraterrestrial intelligence from the future. This being claimed he did not have a name, as names were no longer used because the whole society was telepathic. However, he said he realized we needed a name for him so he chose the word "Bashar," which in Arabic apparently means the "bringer of good news." While the idea of channeling was still new to me, I wanted to remain open-minded about the subject.

Several months later, in October of 1996, it turned out that Daryl Anka was going to channel Bashar at the Estes Park Star Visions Conference. I went to the conference not knowing what to expect. Daryl proceeded to channel Bashar, who spoke to us about the four laws of the universe (from the perspective of his people which he called the *Essassani*, named after their home-world) and how humans needed to be more holistic and integrated before meeting extraterrestrials like himself in the near future. Bashar said we had to meet ourselves and our "inner aliens" first. While there was no way to prove that Daryl was actually channeling an extraterrestrial, the information seemed interesting and I went back to see his workshop the next day.

Bashar's ideas tended to focus on the physics of how we create our own reality and why life is, in actuality, a holographic mirror of ourselves. The intensity and conviction with which Bashar spoke made him seem all the more credible. Bashar also generally devoted a lot of time to answering people's individual questions, and that is how the Hale-Bopp issue was brought up.

After the conference I purchased tapes of the channeling sessions from Bashar's weekly meetings in the L.A. area. It turned out that in November of 1996, someone had asked Bashar about our viewings of the Hale-Bopp companion object. Were the viewings correct and what was really out there? Bashar stated unequivocally that we had misinterpreted our data and the original sighting itself was a misidentification, probably of a star behind the comet at the time that Chuck Sramek took his photo. Thus there was no companion object, just a comet coming very close to the Earth. The RV sessions simply reflected the historical significance of the Hale-Bopp comet in our collective consciousness.

Having been under the impression that there was a companion object, this information was quite a shock to me, especially since it came from an apparently extraterrestrial source. However, Bashar's analysis seemed accurate and given that there was no visual sighting of the object after the comet came out from behind the sun, I concluded that he was right. What we had all learned was to be more careful in interpreting our viewing sessions and take more time before drawing conclusions from the data.

On another interesting note, in the summer of 1998, Bashar mentioned the strong possibility of a terrorist attack on New York and other American cities. At the time, Bashar talked about the possibility of a small nuclear device being used in the attack. While this did not literally come to pass on September 11, 2001, many of the specifics he talked about did come true, especially with regard to the other cities involved, perpetrators' modes of operation, and the general resulting effect on our mass consciousness. This lends more support of the relevancy of channeling to our study of subtle energies.

Extraterrestrial Opponent Groups

If doing viewing sessions on extraterrestrials was a new adventure to begin with, things at the Farsight Institute took an even stranger twist when people there determined that negative extraterrestrials existed who were opposed to Earth and the Galactic Federation, the organization that supposedly oversees our section of the universe. The negative beings were apparently similar to reptiles and were very strictly authoritarian and oriented towards domination. Where this information came from was unclear, but that is the nature of rumors. These descriptions were also consistent with the general portrayals of reptilian ETs focused around UFO literature.

Whatever the original source of the information was, we soon became convinced that this ET opposition group was a serious threat to the well-being of the Farsight Institute and the Earth as a whole. We also thought that this group was responsible for the Hale-Bopp debacle. In our minds, we thought we had the perfect tool to fight this galactic evil: our remote viewing skills. Soon after, we began viewing this opposition group, to learn everything we could about them. The target cue would generally be some variant of the "ET opposition group to the Earth and the Galactic Federation." Courtney also believed that the Galactic Federation itself had given the Farsight Institute an ET assistant to help us with our viewing. In theory, this ET helper could allow us to breach security apparatuses set up by our ET reptile opponents to prevent us from viewing them. We would then penetrate deep into reptile space to learn about their evil plans for galactic domination and subjugation of the human race.

If there was ever a group storyline going amongst an organization of trainer viewers, this was it. The scary thing was that, in my view, many of us were serious about it. Some believed that spies had been sent by the reptiles to infiltrate the Farsight Institute. Anyone who questioned the motives or operations of the Farsight Institute was considered a potential ally of these enemies. Someone even suggested to me that people I considered my friends were these spies and I should be careful in dealing with them. As a result of these viewpoints, the Institute sank into a frenzy of paranoia from which, in my view, it never recovered. Good people were lost to groundless accusation, and the trust that is so necessary to an organization like Farsight began to evaporate permanently. To be fair to the Farsight Institute, many of us wanted to believe in this scenario because of the excitement it engendered. No one person was to blame, as we all shared in the storyline.

Cosmic Contacts

Many people at Farsight had positive experiences from their participation in RV. A friend of mine, Doris, from central Colorado, awoke one night to find strange lights above her bed. A few nights later she woke again and felt compelled to draw artwork like she had never seen before. This continued for a long time and eventually she called these pictures "soul portraits." She had never had any inclination to create art before and attributed this new found skill to her mind–opening work in RV. Figure 16 represents one of Doris's portraits.

Painting © 2000 by Doris Rannells

Figure 16: An Example of Doris's Soul Portrait Drawings

From Remoteness to Resonance

Whatever the exact nature of channeling is, the entity Bashar had some very interesting ideas about viewing and how it worked. He basically said it was a form of frequency-matching between a person and another person or object of interest. When frequencies of two things match, they spontaneously begin to exchange information through etheric levels of reality. Thus, RV was not a remote process at all, but a process of "resonance identification." Everything that exists has resonance and once that resonance is identified it can be perceived from anywhere in the universe. This also means that viewing is developed into an innate part of us that anyone can access.

The very idea of "remote viewing" is a bit of an oxymoron if you think about it. According to Targ and Puthoff, the term was coined out of a desire to get government funding, so it had to sound intriguing from the beginning. However, they never thought this was the best term. And in some sense, it is not really viewing at all, but sensing, as some viewers never see their target at all but merely get an indirect sense of it. Mainly, the term implies the idea of perceiving something at a distance from the viewer. The viewer is here; the object is over there.

Yet the modern quantum perspective shows the idea of distance and separation is, in some sense, part of the illusion of physical reality. In reality, all matter is waves that are continually interacting. Therefore, remote viewing is not remote at all, but a form of resonance matching such as a radio. All frequencies surround a radio, but it only picks up what it is tuned to. In the same way, the viewer's intent sets up a field of communication between the object, person, or place of interest and the viewer's awareness. Just like two tuning forks ringing when only one of them is struck, when two things are in resonance, they transmit information back and forth. For this reason, I feel that the term *resonant viewing* more accurately describes this process. However, unlike electromagnetic signals, this viewing "signal" does not degrade with distance or time, suggesting that it is a non-local, quantum signal beyond ordinary space-time.

All of the data from our research indicates that everyone has an innate ability to fine tune their own resonance so as to pick up "distant" information. It is not a question of learning how to resonant. Everyone already knows, intuitively, how to do this. It is more a question of learning how to consciously alter our internal frequencies to match those of people and things that we want to interact with. This opens up new pathways of communications and understanding that we are just coming to grips with, at least in modern times.

Since the scientific revolution of several hundred years ago, our culture has become increasingly focused on "hard," empirical information that can be easily measured and verified. Subtle, resonant energies, while challenging to measure with traditional physics equipment, appear to be the cutting edge of new sciences. While very "soft" in a sense, they are also non-local, which adds a whole new dimension to this area of inquiry. They have the potential to provide new avenues to energies and frequencies we have yet to understand and promise to open new door ways to the infinite.

Link—An Extraterrestrial Viewing Odyssey

On October 15, 1996, a clinical psychologist from the University of Washington, Jonathan Bradley Rutter, was allegedly walking with his dog in the Washington Cascade mountains. He suddenly encountered a non-ordinary life form and a violent encounter ensued. His dog apparently attacked the creature and was turned to ash. In his panic, Rutter hit the creature on the head and thought he had killed it. Thinking it was dead, he then took the being home and, not knowing what else to do, put it in his freezer. Subsequent events changed his life forever. The details of his story are recounted in his book, *Link—An Extraterrestrial Odyssey* (1998), using the pseudonym "Dr. Jonathan Reed" and co-written with Robert Raith. More information is also available on the websites www.OdysseyLink.net and www.AlienDestiny.com. This accidental encounter apparently involved a being and a black obelisk-shaped craft, pictured below.

Rutter had a video camera and a 35mm still camera at the time and took the photo shown below in Figure 17. Independent analysis by two different film laboratories confirms the veracity of the photo. Rutter believes the "obelisk" in the photo has the function of *linking* two realities, rather than acting as a transportation vehicle. When he physically touched the object it seemed immovable, as if it were rigidly fixed to that specific location in the forest.

Photo © 1998 by Jonathan Rutter

Figure 17: Rutter's "Obelisk"

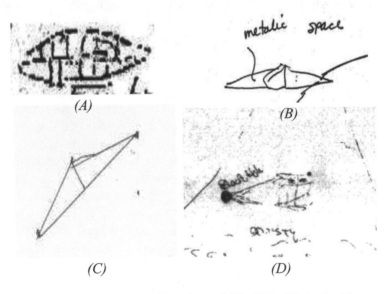

Figure 18: Viewers' Sketches of Obelisk: Note that in sketch (D), viewer describes tip of object as a "black hole."

In 1998 and '99, I gave this target to our advanced viewers under controlled type-4 conditions, meaning they had no knowledge in advance what they were viewing. I wanted to see what types of information they would come up with. The previous pictures (Figure 18) were drawn by some of the viewers and, in my view, indicate their viewing contact with a real object.

These sessions indicate that the encounter was either a real event or a representation of something real, as many of the viewers described the same type of phenomena: an interdimensional reconnaissance vehicle, a frightening encounter, and strange energies. In the sketch above, the viewer draws an object hovering above the ground and labels it as a black hole. Also, many of the viewers started having telepathic encounters with the being, nicknamed "Freddy" by Rutter, after doing the viewing sessions. Some of the viewers also had the feeling that the encounter was observed by other beings from a distance so as to study Rutter and Freddy's reactions to each other.

In the Spring of 2002, it became known that Rutter had written his book under a false name. Many of the details of his story were then also called into question. From the author's own research it appears that Rutter did indeed have a real encounter but then, for some inexplicable reason, invented some of the people and incidents associated with the event. One of the people mentioned in his book died many years before the events in the book occurred. However the veracity of other characters has been confirmed by investigators. The detail in the video evidence seems compelling and would be very expensive to fabricate as would be the physical artifacts associated with the case. Readers are encouraged to use their discernment when studying this affair. They may find out more about the story, and ongoing research about its credibility and accuracy, at the websites mentioned above.

6. Liquid Landscapes:
The Mystery of Crop Formations

MY FIRST INTRODUCTION TO CROP circles began at the
Farsight Institute during an advanced RV session. Towards the end
of a week-long training we were given blind (hidden) pictures of
crop circles. These included the 1996 Stonehenge and Windmill Hill
formations (Figures 19 and 20) as viewing targets. During the
session, my first impression was of a spaceship coming from the
Earth's outer atmosphere over a field and then releasing some sort
of powerful energy into the crop. Other people in the class drew
exact replicas of the formations. The whole topic was new and it
seemed quite a mystery. These initial RV sessions convinced me
there was something uniquely important in the topic. My sessions
included references to strange energies and star colonies

About two weeks after I returned from the RV training, I went
off to a UFO conference in Denver. This was the first UFO
conference I had ever attended and I did not know what to expect.
I was surprised to find very few people wearing Vulcan ears; instead,
there was much serious discussion about the subject matter. One of
the lectures I attended was given by Ron Russell, who presented a
slide show dealing with crop circles. I thought that I would finally
get some definitive information about what those formations were,
who was making them, and why. However, Ron presented the
subject matter as if no one knew the answers to these questions.
According to Ron, even though there were some witnesses to the
formation of simple circles, the phenomena as a whole was an enig-
ma.

Photo © 1996 by Ron Russell

Figure 19: Julia Set Formation, near Stonehenge, 1996

Photo © 1996 by Busty Taylor

Figure 20: Triple Julia Formation, Windmill Hill, 1996

For several years I studied this topic as diligently as I could. Beginning in 1997 and again in 1998, I went with Ron on one of his crop circle tours in Wiltshire, England. For two weeks, we heard lectures from resident experts on the subject. If possible, we would go into newly formed circles with these experts who would explain how they were made and their significance. Some of the theories included UFOs, Earth energies, and atmospheric discharges. The height of the experience was the Glastonbury Crop Circle Symposium, which has been held every July since 1991 in the medieval town of Glastonbury, England.

The Avebury 3D Cubes of 1999

Since I began studying the subject in 1996, I was aware of rumors circulating that the circles were mostly manmade. Various groups and names were put forth, but these people rarely came forward to claim credit for a particular formation. The exceptions were the public demonstrations, such as the Avebury 3D Cubes formation in 1999 (Figure 21). This formation, commissioned by the *Daily Mail* newspaper with the permission of the Farthing family, on whose land it appeared, was a creation of the Circle Makers—a four-man team of graphics artists, mostly from London, who have been making crop circles since the early 1990s (www.CircleMakers.org). The formation appeared on the night of a full moon, leading many to argue that any humans in a field next to the popular tourist destination of Avebury would have been seen. Researcher Chad Deetken and his wife went for a walk around the area at 1:30 a. m. and did not see anything suspicious. The newspaper interviewed people on the day the formation appeared, asking them about its authenticity. Many interviewees believed that no human could do such a thing, and this was exactly the sort of comment the newspaper was looking for. The *Daily Mail* wanted to show that people could be fooled. Interestingly, in the interview with the human facilitators of this formation, one of them said, they occasionally saw extremely strange lights while creating formations. In particular, they described that while making a crop circle one night, a bright light lit up in the formation to the extent that all of the participants hit the ground in fear. These human "hoaxers" admitted to observing paranormal effects while making their formations.

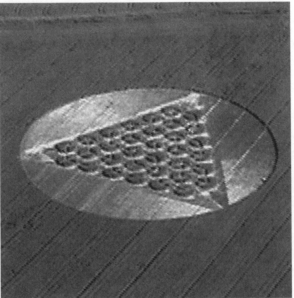

Figure 21: Avebury 3D Cubes Formation

Anomalous Evidence

Though some crop circle researchers had always suspected a large human component to the phenomena, it was difficult to know the truth. At conferences like Glastonbury, however, there were plenty of presentations to suggest just the opposite case—that the human component in crop formations was minimal and that most formations were genuinely mysterious. To back up this claim of non-human involvement, there were many eyewitness accounts of genuinely strange phenomena.

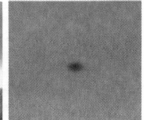

(B) Telegraph Hill
(close-up)

(A) Telegraph Hill

Photo © 1995 by Jilaen Sherwood

Figure 22: Telegraph Hill UFO

In 1997, David Kingston, a former British military intelligence officer, presented his own experience of watching UFOs over Clay Hill near Warminster with a large group in the late 1970s and then seeing simple circle-like formations right below the area the next morning. Kingston's UFO experience began in the British military, where he was assigned to investigate UFO encounters and incidents for the Ministry of Defense. During this period, Kingston became convinced that UFOs were real. In 1998, Kingston showed several photographs, taken weeks apart, of the 1995 Telegraph Hill formation, all appearing to show a small flying disk above the formation. The photo in Figure 22 was taken by Jilaen Sherwood and shows a similar object. Also, I was shown another photo of the same formation, taken by conference regular Chris Hopper of the U.K. regarding the same formation. The photo, taken around the same time as Kingston's photos, shows the same disk-like object.

In 1999, Kingston also played tapes of strange trilling noises recorded by Colin Andrews and others in various formations. NASA has analyzed these sounds and determined they are mechanical, not natural, in origin. To this date, nobody knows what those sounds are. This type of evidence suggests that something truly odd is associated with the circle phenomena.

In July of 1999, I personally had my own weird experience in the so-called Devil's Den formation in Fyfield Downs near Avebury (Figure 23). I had spotted Japanese researcher and author Masao Maki on his way down from the parking area and we walked down together in the early evening. Maki had originally become a crop circle researcher after studying other subjects, such as the gurus in India, and the Dr. Fritz psychic surgery phenomenon in Brazil. Professionally, Maki was known as something of a debunker, a "guru buster," though he had determined that the Dr. Fritz phenomena were real (see his book *Quantum Surgeon: The Quest for Brazil's Psychic Surgeon*). After studying crop circles, Maki became intrigued by the subject and had been coming to England for several years.

Upon approaching the Devil's Den formation in July 1999, Maki's new Sony digital camcorder began to malfunction, with a blinking light to indicate that the tape heads were dirty. Then his camera froze up, which was also odd because it was a brand-new camera. This should have alerted me to what was going on, but I was too eager to go into this intriguing formation that had appeared next to an old Neolithic dolmen. I went on alone, while Maki attempted to fix his camera, which started working again a few minutes later.

Upon approaching the edge of the formation, my Trek-520 electrostatic detector went haywire; the meter got stuck at -0.03 volts. When I tested the batteries later, they were completely drained of electricity.

I had been experimenting with this device in hopes of replicating John Burke's results from the early 1990s. Burke, a member of the BLT team consisting of himself, Nancy Talbott, and Dr. William Levengood, had found some interesting electrostatic anomalies with this device in several fresh circles.

(A) Devil's Den at Fyfield Down

*(B) The Author with
Trek-520 Device*

*(C) Trek Malfunction in Devil's
Den Formation*

Figure 23: ES Meter Malfunction in Crop Formation

(A) Hackpen   Photo © 1999 by Author

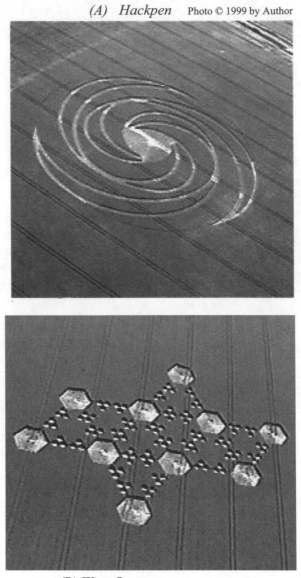

(B) West Overton   Photo © 1999 by Ron Russell

Figure 24: Hackpen and West Overton Formations, 1999

These formations appeared to have a small positive charge early in the morning, when the reading should have been slightly negative, representing the Earth's natural background charge. For Burke, these readings suggested that some unknown force was involved in the formations, something not created by simple mechanical means.

Ron Russell, who had arrived earlier in the summer, also had some astounding results with the device. Upon entering two previous formations, the West Overton Octahedron and the Hackpen Vortex (Figure 24), the Trek-520 had instantly frozen and the battery drained in seconds. Other formations had no effect on the meter. There is a real mystery as to why some formations affect the meter and others do not. The static meter was able to pick up some energy signature from these formations that was different from the surrounding grain fields. In the Devil's Den formation, however, there is no doubt that the meter had reacted in an extreme way. As my electrostatic detecting device froze at the edge of the Devil's Den formation, I became very excited as I knew something anomalous was at work here. On the outside of the formation, the meter had worked as normal, but now on the edge it failed. Crossing into the formation, the meter remained jammed and would not work for the rest of the evening, even after it was turned on and off several times.

It took until the next morning for the device and battery to recover. In the meantime, Maki had now joined me in the formation. We spent some time walking around in the sunset enjoying the spectacular design. His camera was working again, or at least so he thought. About fifteen minutes later we noticed that both our cameras batteries were draining rapidly. This was evident because our Sony cameras used so-called "info-Lithium" batteries, where the viewfinder displayed the remaining number of minutes left in the battery. While both our batteries were near fully charged when we came into the formation, they now had only a few minutes of power left. We had only been there twenty minutes, with most of that time spent on looking around rather than filming. To top it all off, Rob Speight of the Internet site www.TheNoiseRoom.com, a site devoted to paranormal topics, also came into the formation to take photos. He then noticed that his GPS device, which only minutes before had fourteen hours of battery life left, was now dead (Figure 25). Upon taking the batteries out, he found they were completely discharged. It was apparent that something strange was happening. In fact, I later learned that Dr. Patricia Hill, who owns the same type of Sony video camera, experienced damage to her Lithium batteries that lasted for approximately one year after entering the same formation. The batteries would hold no more than a small charge, even after hours of recharging.

These types of experiences have been reported around crop formations for decades. You might think it's all folklore until you experience it yourself. I was with Ron Russell in 1997 in the Danebury Triad formation when he put his Sony Hi8 camera down on the ground for a moment. It never worked again that summer. When Ron took it to a Sony repair facility, they said the transformer solder joints had melted and charged him $300 for repairs. In 1998, I experienced camera failure two days in row. My first experience was while taking pictures of crop formations in the Alton Barnes area at a distance from the East Field seven-sided Snowflake formation, when my Olympus film camera rewound on its own after only four pictures had been taken (figure 26). The second was in the Lockeridge "Hydra" formation the next day, where my camera rewound the film again without anyone having pressed the rewind button.

(A) GPS Device Fails

(B) Drained Batteries from GPS Device

Video Frames © 1999 by author.
**Figure 25: GPS Device Failure in
Devil's Den Crop Formation.**

*(A) Lockeridge Formation, Where My
Camera Malfunctioned*

*(B) East Field Formation: The Site of Another
Camera Malfunction*

Photos © 1998 by Ron Russell

Figures 26: Lockeridge and East Field Formations, 1998

UFOs and Manmade Formations

Alton Barnes has always been the center of unusual paranormal activity. Hence, anomalous camera failure isn't surprising. The area is overlooked by several hills: Adam's Grave, Knapp Hill, and Golden Ball Hill (a name given to the hill for the balls of light that are frequently seen there).

In early July of 1998, I was on Knapp Hill, in the evening gazing around at the area. It was a fairly quiet night, and I decided to leave at around 10:00 p.m. Walking down the hill onto the main pathway near the parking lot I ran into two couples looking at stars through a telescope. The Russian space station "Mir" was especially visible that night, and we had all seen it passing overhead a few minutes earlier. One of the couples told me they had once been parked on Pewsey Road, below, looking for strange anomalies at night. A police car happened to see them and stopped to ask what they were up to. The police man was no stranger to the area and told the couple he had once been cruising down Knapp Hill toward Alton Barnes in the early morning hours when three balls of light rushed towards his car, circled around for a moment, and then shot off into the distance as one coherent ball.

In 1990, photographer Steve Alexander was sitting up on Milk Hill when he spotted a ball of light moving across the field toward a nearby formation below Milk Hill. The ball of light actually appeared to explore the formation before moving across the field and over a tractor, which then stalled. The driver of the tractor remembers seeing the ball as a brightly lit beach ball. What is odd is that the farmer didn't know why the diesel tractor, which has no electronics in it, stopped. Moreover, after the tractor stopped, it then started again on its own. Steve recorded much of this incident on video.

Another ball of light story relates to the '99 Koch and Kyborg formation near Woodborough Hill, next to Alton Barnes. Dr. Achim Koch and Hans Jurgen Kyborg, two German researchers, were interested in using crop formations to communicate with the unknown. In the mid-1990s Koch and Kyborg made the discovery

Figure 27: Koch and Kyborg Formation 1999.

Photo ©1999 by Author

Ball of Light Close-up

Photo ©1999 by Hans Niehaus

Figure 28: Ball of Light Seen Near Koch and Kyborg Formation

that some of the ancient pyramids in Egypt were related to a particular set of constellations in the sky. These constellations also appeared to be related to many crop formations. On the basis of this information, Koch and Kyborg reasoned that crop circles might be a form of communication from an extraterrestrial intelligence. Each summer, Koch and Kyborg make formations on Tim Carson's land in Alton Barnes with the intent of communicating with this intelligence. In 1999, they created a formation shown in Figure 27, and then led a group meditation on Woodborough Hill a few days later. Hans Niehaus happened to be on Knapp Hill earlier in the day and saw a ball of light moving across the land. He managed to photograph it just before it disappeared (Figure 28). These balls of light are seen frequently in this area and seem to be especially centered around crop formations.

In July of 2000, Peter Sorensen was flying over a formation near Bishops Cannings when he caught an anomalous object on videotape (Figure 29). It wasn't until he showed the footage to an audience at a conference in Andover the following August that someone noticed the object and asked him to play back the video again. Upon closer inspection, the object seems unexplainable with our current state of knowledge. There are no wings present on the object, which doesn't leave much else in the way of explanation. The sequence below shows the still images of the object taken over a few seconds.

While the balls of light may be dismissed by some as unknown electromagnetic phenomena, they often appear to possess some innate intelligence in their movements. In several of the known sightings of these objects, they appear to move deliberately in and out of nearby formations. Whether the balls of light are guided probes or living organisms of some sort remains to be seen.

Video frames © 2000 by Peter Sorensen

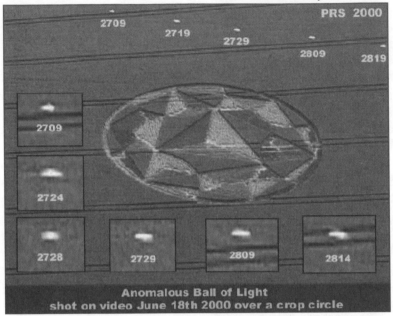

Figure 29: Anomalous Object Over Formation

In July of 1999, I decided to go up to Woodborough Hill, near Alton Barnes, for the evening at approximately 9:00 p.m. Linda Moulton Howe, the well-known journalist of the paranormal, and I had just finished eating dinner at the Wagon and Horses in nearby Beckhampton. Linda decided to come with me.

We drove out across the Carsons' land and walked up to the top of the hill. Shortly after arriving there, we noticed a sparkling blue light that appeared to flicker on and off several times per second. It seemed to be slightly behind Knapp Hill, about one mile northwest of us. The sparkling pattern appeared random: first it was bright, then dimmer, then very bright. It also appeared to jump around in the sky over an area of a few hundred feet. After watching for ten minutes or so, it finally disappeared.

Chad Deetken, the Canadian researcher, had also been watching the object from his patio balcony in Alton Barnes. He first saw it in a field to the west and believed it was a police strobe light on top of a patrol car. The light then lifted off the field and moved over to the area where we had first seen it.

A Japanese TV crew also filmed the object from across the valley on the hill, Adam's Grave. They followed the object in their car as it moved around the Alton Barnes area. Zooming in, it appeared to be small balls pressed together, blinking and sparkling. They followed it in their car until it sporadically faded away (Figure 30).

The object ended up right over an area where a formation appeared the next morning in West Kennett. The formation appeared built around squares and was almost certainly manmade. I later found out that the object was probably a set of helium-filled balloons with a strobe light in the center. It was conceived and sent up by one part of the Japanese film crew to see how their colleagues stationed on Adam's Grave would react. Though not a genuine UFO sighting, the incident is representative of the types of weird experiences people can have around crop circles.

(A) Close-up of Object
Photo © 1999 by Nippon TV

(B) Kennett Formation
Formation Photo © 1999 by Author

Figure 30: "Mysterious" Object and Associated Formation

Tawsmeade Copse

One of the most interesting stories I have heard about balls of lights involves the wooded area in England known locally as the Taws-meade Copse, just between the villages of West Stowell and Alton Barnes in Wiltshire. According to my information, a team of human circle makers went into this field in early August with the intent of making a formation. They walked into the field and made several construction lines to outline the entire formation. As they did, they noticed three balls of light moving in their direction. The balls of light settled around them at the edges of the field. There was something ominous about the balls of light; they began to get the feeling that they should soon leave which they did.

Several days later, on August 9th, 1998, another circle-making team, I am told, approached the same area at night and constructed a formation with seven-fold geometry 400 feet across (Figure 31). A brother and sister were out star watching on nearby Adam's Grave, and at approximately 1 a.m. they saw a ball of light come down the Pewsey Valley and move through the Tawsmeade Copse area—over the exact location of the circle-making team. The ball then split into three smaller balls and moved over the field. The balls left the area and then reappeared back several times until approximately 4:00 a.m. The sister described them to me as headlights moving over the field, at times about the speed of a fast car, but not projecting light in any specific direction. Another pair of women on neighboring Knapp Hill that night reported seeing the same thing.

These stories provide anecdotal evidence that mysterious phenomena are associated with crop formations and that these phenomena, in some cases, demonstrated a deliberate intelligence. An incident of this sort was recorded over the Barbury Castle formation of 1999 in August (Figure 32). An English tourist, Donald Fletcher, happened to be videotaping the formation when a slow-moving ball of light appeared perhaps twenty feet over the formation, which had people walking in it (Figure 33A).

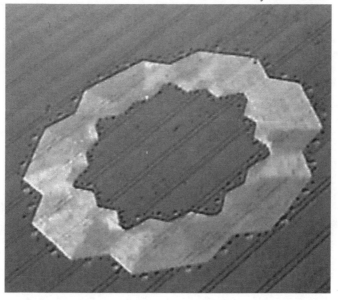

Figure 31: Tawsmeade Copse Formation, 1998

The ball then made a sharp 70-degree turn and sped off to the north, disappearing over some farm sheds. According to my own calculations using a map and the video time code, it was moving at approximately 180 mph while at top speed (Figure 33B).

Another type of information comes from photographs of these formations. Many photographs show strange anomalies like shafts of light or UFOs. Ron Russell took a group photo in the previously mentioned Danebury Triad formation in 1997 which clearly shows a small, black disk overhead. This might suggest that these crop formations attract anomalies.

Figure 32: Barbury Castle Formation 1999

Veteran researcher Colin Andrews told me a story of two men who ventured into the Chilbolton formation in 1998, the same place that received the well-publicized "Face" and "Arecibo" formations in 2001. First they were chased out by bees and then by bats. On their third attempt to visit the formation that evening, they saw a glowing red ball over the formation and encountered four men in a white van that had clustered antennas on its roof.

The men told them to leave the area. There are many similar stories, and they suggest that some formations associated with real anomalies are monitored by someone.

(A)

(B) Video Frames © 1999 by Donald Fletcher

**Figure 33: Anomalous Ball of Light
over Barbury Formation**

What are the Balls of Light?

Some scientists have suggested that balls of light are related to ball lightning, a phenomenon that is often associated with the movement of tectonic plates in advance of an earthquake. Perhaps the plethora of balls of light seen in and around the Wiltshire area are associated with this type of natural process? The problem with this explanation is that the luminous objects seen near crop formations appear to be intelligently controlled. In the case of Steve Alexander's ball of light, it appeared to explore one formation and then skipped to another nearby. It then caused a tractor to stall for approximately thirty seconds as it passed overhead. The tractor driver said it looked like a glowing beach ball. In the Barbury '99 formation, the object made an abrupt turn right over the formation and then sped off. In another instance, a group of German tourists witnessed a ball of light make five passes over and through a crop formation.

In several cases, some on video tape, military helicopters are seen to approach balls of light over crop formations and attempt to chase them away. In one instance related to me by Colin Andrews, the balls of light appeared to do a dance around two military helicopters before speeding off.

Often strange lights appear around crop formations that do not appear as coherent shapes. The photo in Figure 34 was taken by a Japanese tourist in the summer of 2000, who saw the shape before photographing it.

Another interesting photograph was taken by Nick Nicolson who resides in England. He didn't see the anomaly in Figure 35 when he took the photograph; he only noticed later. It appears to be like smoke, but it is coming from above the crop. These types of phenomena are regularly seen around crop formations.

Figure 34: Anomalous Light in Crop Formation

Figure 35: Mysterious Light near Crop Formation

We don't know what these objects are, but the evidence suggests that they are not solely the product of electrostatic Erth energies and plate movements. Perhaps the crop formations activate energy fields that we have yet to fully understand.   For more information about this topic,please see Linda Moulton Howe's book *Mysterious Lights and Crop Circles* (2000), and Eltjo Hasellhoff's, *The Deepening Complexity of Crop Circles* (2001).

Summer 2000

The summer of 2000 began like any other crop circle season with a few formations in April and June and then a flurry in July and August. For myself, however, this circle season was like no other. I had come to England that year with the intent of getting to the bottom of the mystery and in many respects I did. Towards the end of July, Ron Russell and myself, as well as Peter Sorensen and Linda Moulton Howe, were offered the opportunity to watch a daytime, legal formation being made by Matthew Williams and Paul Damon, two veteran circle makers, for a television Internet commercial. Williams and Damon had begun like the rest of us, with an interest in the phenomena. They had spent many a night on hilltops surrounding the Wiltshire area looking for signs of paranormal activity in the fields. After many cold evenings, they decided to independently start experimenting with circle-making. For them, it was like answering some unknown intelligence in its own language. In other words, a paranormal dialogue.

Soon they found they were getting plenty of paranormal contact out in the fields at night including balls of light and UFO sightings. Williams and Damon concluded that manmade formations were an important part of the whole phenomena. Unlike the English hoaxers Doug and Dave of the 1980s, they were not intent on deceiving or debunking the phenomena as much as facilitating contact with the unknown and creating circles for other researchers to study. One of Williams' best creations was the Basket at Bishops Cannings in 1999 (Figure 36.).

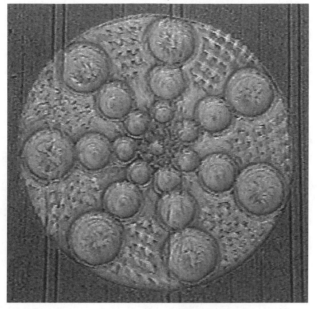

Figure 36: Basket Formation, Bishops Cannings, 1999

We were offered the chance to see a formation being created in the daytime and took them up on it. The location was outside Potterne, near Devizes in Wiltshire. The pattern took the shape of an "r" inside an "@" sign. We assembled the morning of July 23rd, went out to the site, and had the farmer lead us to the chosen area.

We spent several hours watching Matthew, Paul, and their assistant, Andy, make the formation with so-called "stomper boards" which are planks of wood wrapped in tape, to prevent damage to the plant. Ropes are attached to the boards to help the circle makers create an "up and down" stomping motion into the wheat with their feet. The boards are used to "stomp" the plants into in a pattern.

I was given the plans ahead of time. As the formation was made in the daylight, Matthew and Paul made "on the fly" calculations of distances and angles inside the formation. This was interesting because most researchers thought it was impossible for people to create large, even-looking formations like this one (Figure 37). The "r" formation was completed at a leisurely pace in less than five hours.

Photo © 2000 by Author.

**Figure 37: Matthew Williams Making
the"r" Formation, Potterne, 2000**

(A) R Sketch

(B) R Formation

Photos © 2000 by Author

Figure 38: Diagram of Potterne "r" and Final Formation

In 1997, Michael Glickman, a former architect and long-time crop circle researcher, employed a professional surveying company in the U.S. to estimate how long it would take and how much it would cost to reproduce specific formations such as the Silbury Hill Koch Snowflake fractal and the similar Milk Hill formation. They estimated that, using traditional surveying techniques, it would take them several days, during the day, at the cost of several thousand dollars per formation. From this information, many concluded that no group of people, in the dead of night, could make such a formation in five hours or less. The Potterne formation, though relatively small, proved this viewpoint wrong. For it was obviously not necessary to survey the field ahead of time (Figure 38); it could be done by improvising with a sketch, surveyor's tape, a calculator, and bamboo stakes.

This experience showed us that humans could indeed make a formation with all the trimmings that were previously thought to be signs of "authentic" formations: those made by extraterrestrials or Earth energies. These included swirled ground lay of the plants, magically standing stalks, and bent stems. More importantly, our electrostatic meter, the Trek-520 device, showed high readings, indicating that the formation was changing the flow of energy in the field. We had previously thought that high ES readings were a sign of authenticity: the Koch and Kyborg formations of '99, made in Tim Carson's field with his permission, exhibited no such electrostatic charges. But the Potterne data proved us wrong again: manmade formations could also exhibit strong electrostatic anomalies. This "R" pattern, however, was done in the daytime and doing it at night would be an entirely different matter. Would the effects be the same?

Several weeks later, I was offered the chance to see a formation made at night in the Cherhill area. The number of people involved in this formation totaled seven, including some who had come from far away just for the event. In this case, the farmer was not paid, and I knew this a few hours in advance of the event. Although for legal and ethical reasons I would have preferred to witness a paid formation, my personal curiosity was so strong that I went along along to watch along to watch anyway. I wanted to see whether a group of human circle-makers could really accomplish such a formation in under six hours in total darkness. The sketch was shown to me ahead of time. The actual pattern used by the circle-makers during the night to create the formation is shown below (Figure 39). The formation ending up taking approximately five hours to construct and was done in green barley (Figure 40). It was quite a thrill to be out there at night. The leaders of the group had made all the calculations ahead of time. In the still quiet of the Wiltshire nighttime, I watched as measurements were taken, bamboo stakes were put into the ground, construction lines laid out, and eventually a pattern was impressed by the use of wooden "stomper boards" into the grain (Figure 41).

Figure 39: Sketch Used by Circle-Makers at Night to Construct the Cherhill 2000 Formation

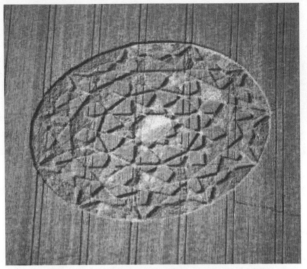

Figure 40: Cherhill Formation, 2000
Photo © 2000 by Colin Andrews

**Figure 41: Circle-Maker in Cherhill
Formation** Video Frame © 2000 by Author

Many researchers believe it is impossible to do such work at night because of the darkness. However, having been at this circle-making event the entire night, I can say there is enough light in the Wiltshire countryside to see what you are doing. The area is surrounded by cities and military bases which give off enough light to reflect off the clouds and back down into the fields. It only takes about half an hour for your eyes to adjust to these conditions. Given the methods that human circle-makers use, they only need to see about 20 to 30 feet around them to make even a large formation. Dimmed (ie., taped) LED flashlights are occasionally used to look at the printed pattern. Handheld two-way radios are also useful for communicating over large distances.

During the course of the night, the group of circle-makers experienced a time anomaly: at one point all their watches appeared to read 2:45 a.m. and then a few moments later, all the watches read 2:00 a.m. I could not verify this apparent time reversal as I was not wearing a watch, but it does underscore the possibility of the spooky time-and-space shifting effects of crop formations. The following day, measurements with the Trek-520 device showed strong electrostatic charges within the formation.

Ron Russell recounted a similar experience several years earlier where he was walking in the nearby Avebury Trusloe area at night, away from a CSETI skywatch led by Dr. Steven Greer. He was headed towards his car to get some film, saw a campfire in the distance and approached it. He perceived people dressed in ancient garb that would have been appropriate 500 years ago. They seemed out of place and talked in a rough, Chaucerian dialect. He then walked back to his skywatch group. Though it seemed like he had been gone for an hour, he had only been away from his group for a few minutes.

The West Overton Formation of 2000
Later in the summer, Matthew Williams made another formation to show the research community that humans had the ability to make convincingly well-constructed formations. A few months earlier on Whitley Strieber's "Dreamland" show, broadcast across

North America every Sunday night on radio, Williams had heard Michael Glickman say that it was nearly impossible for a human person to create a seven-sided formation. Thus Williams set out to prove Glickman wrong.

He sent Whitley, myself, and Ron Russell the plans for the formation a few days in advance (Figure 42). He also notified me of the location just before he made the formation. Unfortunately the wheat was somewhat old by the end of August so the resulting formation did not look all that great. Part of the central detail was messy as a result of tramlines (farm tracks used by tractors) that ran through the formation. Nonetheless, the formation showed that humans could make seven-sided formations.

(A)Diagram of 7 Fold Formation Sketch © 2000 by Matthew Williams

(B)West Overton 2000
Photo © 2000 by Peter Sorensen

Figure 42: West Overton Formation, 2000, and Sketch

Even though this was intended by Matthew Williams to be a public demonstration, he hadn't sought the farmer's permission. Michael Glickman then pressed the police to arrest Matthew on charges of criminal trespassing and vandalism. The emails Matthew had sent to Whitley before making the formation were introduced into the court record as evidence against him. The farmer, on the behest of some of the more fundamentalist researchers, also signed a written complaint. Williams was eventually fined 140 pounds for the West Overton formation and the Basket formation of '99 which Williams voluntarily admitted to.

The Moire Patterns

The so-called "Moire patterns" were some of the summer of 2000's most spectacular designs. One at Avebury Trusloe, put down in late August, looked like the Earth's magnetic field. Another one completed at Woodborough Hill resembled a Sunflower. Other related patterns were done at West Kennett and Windmill Hill. Interestingly, these four patterns had all appeared on the same page in a book by John Wilson published by Dover seventeen years earlier, *Mosaic and Tesselated Patterns: How to Create Them* (Figure 43). This page was sent to videographer Peter Sorensen in early June by an anonymous source. This type of evidence suggests that the most complex patterns are created by humans, although many crop circle enthusiasts (sometimes known as "croppies") dispute this point. If these complicated formations are done by humans, it implies that any of the intricate crop circles in the past could also have been human-facilitated.

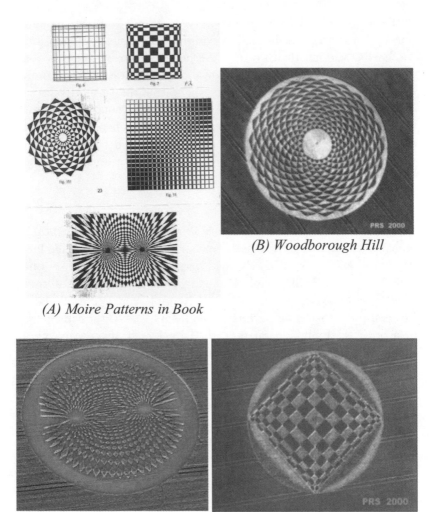

(A) Moire Patterns in Book

(B) Woodborough Hill

(C) Avebury Trusloe

(D) Windmill Hill

Photos © 2000 by Peter Sorensen and Author

Figure 43: Book Patterns and the Moire Formations

Resonant Viewing in Crop Formations

People visiting crop formations often have clairvoyant experiences. In July 1997, Stacy Tussel was inside the beautiful formation at Upham (Figure 44). She decided to sit down and draw the formation. Suddenly, she saw a glimpse of a shape in her mind's eye and drew it on the left side of the paper (Figure 45). To her surprise, a formation very similar to her minds's-eye drawing appeared the next day at Oliver's Castle (Figure 46).

Photo © 1997 by Ron Russell

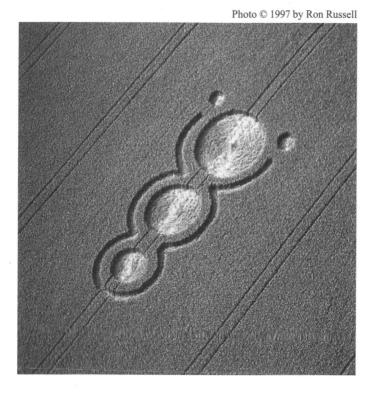

Figure 44: Upham Formation, 1997

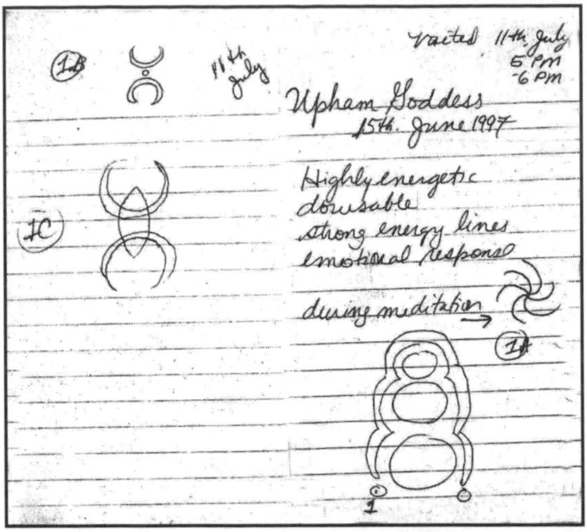

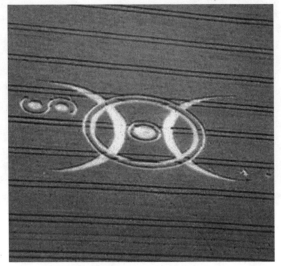

Figure 45: Stace Tussel RV Drawing

Figure 46: Oliver's Castle Formation, 1997

Why Do Manmade Formations Create Anomalous Energy?

The issue of why manmade formations attract balls of light, UFOs, and other phenomena is an important one. How is it that a pattern created by people or some other force in wheat or barley can attract balls of light or cause batteries to fail? One answer may come from the subject of Cymatics, developed by Swiss scientist Hans Jenny. Cymatics is the study of how sound creates shapes and patterns. When turpentine is put on water or sand on a metal sheet, and then sound is applied, complex and coherent patterns appear. Different frequencies create different shapes. These shapes change and transform as the sound changes. Research into Cymatics also suggests that shapes create sound; it is a two-way mechanism. Therefore it is possible that crop formations, due to their coherent shapes and precise layout, create ultrasonic frequencies that affect our technology like cameras and batteries. The shape itself creates an audible sound that affects our equipment and our bodies.

Another possibility was raised by physicist William Tiller at a conference on Science and Consciousness in Albuquerque, New Mexico, in February 2000, where Tiller discussed the physics of "conditioned spaces." According to Tiller, human consciousness can affect the measurable properties of physical spaces. Experiments with projected meditation energy showed that if a group of people concentrated every day, seven to ten days, on an object or machine, they could change how that thing functioned. When this object was placed next to fruit flies they grew faster. There were also subtle temperature changes in the vicinity of the conditioned object. These effects, while small, were statistically significant, which suggests they were not due to chance. In essence, human consciousness conditions the space to behave differently from an ordinary space.

Perhaps the attention of many people on crop formations, together with their Cymatic properties, creates changes in the physical space of the formation. After all, the formations are planned out for weeks in advance, constructed, and then viewed by thousands of people either in person or over the Internet. The focused attention of a mass amount of people might condition the space of the crop formation, imbuing it with unknown energies and etheric possibilities.

Another possibility, one suggested to me by crop circle researcher Colin Andrews, is that plants have unknown electrical and magnetic properties. When they are in a vertical position they are separated by air. However, when they are pushed down to make a crop formation, they are in a horizontal position and touching each other. The arrangement of various types of wheat or other grain crop plants physically contacting one another may produce energetic changes yet to be understood. Plants act like electrical capacitors, each with their own unique electrical charge. When they are laid down in a coherent fashion, the plants all point in the same direction, their energy may combine and interact in unknown ways. This aggregate electrical activity in living material may produce new types of energy yet to be discovered by science.

Take Me to the Mothership

One of the more interesting aspects of the crop circle phenomenon is the extent to which some people will go to deny human involvement in the construction of crop formations. Despite very clear evidence that humans do indeed facilitate many, perhaps most, of the formations on the planet, certain types of fundamentalist researchers remain in a state of denial. It as if the crop circles represent something sacred and divine that would be denigrated and devalued by human participation. In their minds, the entire process would, in effect, be demystified.

From a sociological perspective, this viewpoint seems based on the idea that crop circles are signs of the existence of extraterrestrials. The crop circles themselves are seen as the calling cards of the extraterrestrials, and the researchers involved feel like they are personally destined to board these beings' motherships. Those of us who research the human side of crop circles are possibly seen as interference in this extraterrestrial contact process. With almost religious-like enthusiasm, serious and methodical researchers are zealously castigated and criticized—not on the basis of their evidence—but simply for taking another point of view from the fundamentalists.

Of course, it is quite possible that crop circles represent a blending of different types of energies, thus allowing the participation of humans and other types of intelligence at the same time. However, the fundamentalist interpretation of crop circles (that formations are beyond the realm of human creation) does not recognize the reality and value of human interaction in the process. They have thus created an untenable position that is completely at odds with the evidence and reality behind the phenomena.

Reconnecting to Earth Energies

One lesson of the crop circles is that human-made formations can create magical effects. One wouldn't normally think that simply pushing down a grain crop would launch people into the realm of the paranormal, but the evidence is clear that something unexplainable things can happen. This suggests the possibility that there is an unseen reality that people connect to when creating sacred geometry in living material. When particular shapes are made with intent, coherency, and precision, unknown electromagnetic and etheric properties come into play. These effects have been observed to such an extent that we should consider the idea that crop formations may reconnect us to a type of intelligence within the planet that has long been forgotten. This intelligence appears to be universally available to anyone who is interested in connecting with it. However, it appears to be hidden from our physical senses regardless of its apparent effects on the physical world.

RV also teaches us that unseen mechanisms or properties allow us to accomplish feats that are technically impossible from a classical physicist's point of view. What RV has in common with human circle-making is that both involve the use of shapes to facilitate a process with a generalized, but unknown outcome. While the circle-makers have a particular shape in plan, once the crop formation is complete, the effects are beyond their control. Similarly, a viewer in an RV session uses ideogram shapes and a written protocol without having an attachment to the outcome. In both phenomena, the process is more important than the outcome. To connect to an inter-dimensional process, one must briefly transcend the ordinary so as to create a bridge to other types of energies and intelligence. This is what Deepak Chopra (teacher of quantum health and healing) refers to as going into the "gap," an inner space of infinite potential that is beyond space-time, a place between thoughts where consciousness emerges.

These practices also make us aware that there is another form of human creativity, an interdimensional form that we may have forgotten, until now. This creativity allows a radically strong connection to the heart of the universe, a universe that echoes with intention, vibration, and intelligence. We seem to be approaching an era where we can consciously interact with the fields of energy and do so in a way that simultaneously allows us to integrate our inner being with that of our natural environment.

Another implication of these activities is our increasing contact with extraterrestrial life forms. It appears that these life forms exist at different frequencies from the ones that we are normally accustomed to. Engaging in frequency-shifting activities like RV and crop circles alters our internal frequencies in subtle (and sometimes not so subtle ways). When we explore these new spectra, we encounter types of energy and information that are novel. To meet the outer aliens, we need to meet our inner ones first.

7. Interfacing with the Unknown:
The Promise of Subtle-Energy Sciences

The Living Membrane of Etheric Energy

THIS BOOK BEGAN WITH a discussion of the impacts of technology on time and the flow of information in the world around us. We noted that where efficiency criteria are put first above all other considerations, as many institutions in our modern society tend to do, the effect is to create increasingly discontinuous interactions and the destruction of information. Events are lifted out of their original natural contexts and placed in global settings. This is seen in electronic systems like cable and satellite television, the Internet, and new cellular phone technology. The net effect of all of this is that certain types of data and information are increasingly available anywhere on the planet. The trade-off results in people becoming increasingly out of touch with their local social and ecological environments. They become more isolated and less aware of what is going on right next to them. Clifford Stoll in *High-Tech Heretic* (1999) noted one study that found for every hour per week spent on the Internet, a person's nearby social circle would shrink by about four percent. Researchers also found an increase in depression by roughly one percent per hour per week spent online. The conclusion is that electronic interaction comes at a price.

On the other hand, it is becoming clear that new forms of "internal technology" are developing those permit people to expand their awareness and cultivate innate abilities that have previously been discounted. These mind tools, embedded as they are in our physiology, make us inherently more aware of our relationship to the Earth and the cosmological contexts in which we live. So in the face of local disintegration, new sources of spontaneous, non-local information are readily available. These sources of information are intrinsically difficult to censor and control and therefore have the potential to create radically new types of communities and social groups. In essence, new forms of human creativity are becoming possible, not only as a result of new technologies, but because people are rediscovering energy systems that have lain dormant for thousands of years.

Reconnecting to Etheric Energies

These advanced forms of human creativity can be seen as an interaction with what can be termed "a living membrane" of intelligence and energy. That a geometric pattern in a grain crop or a simple ideogram on a piece of paper creates links to unseen etheric processes is quite a profound idea. It suggests that we all have the potential to enter a universe of powerful resources and creativity with direct access to an information matrix that is brimming with an untold number of possibilities. The ubiquitous balls of light that we previously discussed may represent the edge of this new world, the forerunners of a new vibrational realm.

One of the main characteristics of these subtle energies is that they are spontaneous and self-organizing. In an RV session, the person's subconscious automatically connects to the target signal line and then the data can flow on its own; the viewer does not need to try to make this happen. In fact, trying to make the data flow often interferes with the process. Similarly, the experiences that people often have in association with crop formations are unpredictable. People who want to experience something unusual in a formation often never do, while uninformed bystanders who have no interest in crop circles sometimes receive the show of their lives. This seems to suggest that subtle energies work with a different agenda than those adopted by our conscious mind. These energies flow along different paths than those we are typically accustomed to.

Our experience also suggests that one can contact these energies more readily by letting go rather than by trying harder. While technological information media are generally built around formal operating systems, spontaneous subtle energy transfer occurs within the intrinsic networks built into our bodies. These process systems work on auto-pilot, and while our conscious minds can coexist with them, they are independent of the analytical mind. This is not to suggest that we have no influence over subtle energies—quite the contrary. It is more to say that principles which underlie their operation are much less mechanistic and much more intentional and spontaneous.

Emotions, Intellect, and Intent

One of the more interesting aspects of research in quantum consciousness is the relative effects of thoughts as compared to feelings. Our educational and scientific paradigms have taught us to value linear, rational thoughts over intuitive, holistic responses. Rational thought appears to be more "solid" and practical than emotional feelings. Yet research in quantum consciousness suggests that feelings can have a stronger effect than left-brain, rational thoughts. Our conditioning towards normalcy, where we keep mental track of our feelings and rigorously control them, has led to a state of fragmentation, whereby our multiplex of personalities and belief systems are unintegrated and uncoordinated. It is almost as if we have a permanent watcher in our mind, looking on with approval or disapproval at all we do, think, or feel. This judgmental entity represents the internalization of society's norms and values that we originally picked up from our parents. Some say by the time we are a few years old we have tens of thousands of messages in our minds that loop endlessly on and on (Deepak Chopra, *Ageless Body, Timeless Mind,* 1998). To access these realms of awareness, we need to bypass the constant judgment and internal dialogue that interferes with our well-being.

In resonant viewing it is precisely the free-flowing association and the full exploration of holistic perceptions that generates extremely accurate results. The conscious mind must relinquish control of our thinking process. In fact, when the conscious mind is less involved, the more data become more accurate. It's as if the conscious mind, in its attempt to be practical and logical, actually cuts us off from the flow of information in ourselves. In exchange for logical precision, we lose continuity and flow. By regaining that internal flow, we access a larger stream of intelligence that links us back to the whole universe.

Internal Intelligence

For a long time, the science of biology was based on the idea that the mind and the body were separate entities. In this view, the brain took care of thinking and the body took care of biological functioning. Recent research by Candice Pert, Ph. D., puts this brain-centered view into doubt. Pert's research suggests that the entire body thinks and communicates with the brain through neurotransmitters such as neuropeptides. These messenger molecules are both received and created in the brain and in the organs of our body, as well as in the immune system cells. Thoughts have specific associated neuropeptides, so in a sense, your body is eavesdropping on your mind all the time. Every thought you have has a chemical consequence in your body.

Research by Michael Gershon (1998), for example, shows that we have a second brain in our gut that thinks, calculates, and feels on its own, independently of the brain in our head. Thus it isn't only the brain that thinks, but our entire body. In a sense, every cell is its own brain. Intelligence is not only in our heads, but dispersed throughout our body.

It goes far beyond our bodies, as we can also say that the entire universe is "thinking" and "feeling" all of the time. To the extent that we are aligned with these universal thoughts, then we can feel our perceptual abilities expand. We receive information from a very broad range of "frequencies" rather than just our socially conditioned mind set. Our individual mind becomes integrated with the universal mind.

What this implies is that our intelligence is a multifaceted complex involving all aspects of our being. To use these abilities in a practical way involves not only traditional mental disciplines, but also that we relinquish control and be involved in the flow, or the "zone" as it is sometimes called. That larger intelligence, even though it is not really outside of us, is not directly accessible from our ego-based, linear mind. This universal mind asks to be engaged from a larger perspective.

Etheric Realities—Bridges to the Zero Point

The various subtle energy phenomena we have been discussing defy conventional physics and even stretch our understanding of quantum mechanics. How is it possible for a person to accurately describe something they can't see? Or for shapes in grain crops to create space-time anomalies? Part of the answer may have to do with what we call "etheric" reality. This is an unseen world of energy and information that is directly correlated with physical reality. This realm of reality apparently moves more quickly than physical reality and exists, frequency wise, just above the physical. It can be thought of as being superimposed on physical reality, though we can't sense it with our normal senses.

In an RV session, the viewer's subconscious is apparently aware of this etheric realm, which contains holographic properties. In other words, space and time do not present barriers to our perception because everything in the universe is instantly accessible in this etheric frequency realm, regardless of where it is. As the viewer sets their intent to view a particular target, the information becomes available to them in the etheric. However, its frequency is too high for the mind to be able to consciously detect. This is apparently not a problem for the subconscious mind processes. Much of a viewing session is devoted to the translation of this information from the subconscious to the conscious mind.

Similarly, in a crop formation, the precise geometry and layout of the formation may activate energies at an etheric level, even though all the observer may see is the physical shape. Each pattern may activate a specific etheric frequency or range of frequencies, which then acts to create contact with specific sources of information. Physicist Norman Friedman (1997) describes this idea in the following manner:

> One way to envision the enormous range of consciousness is to imagine a radio dial with an infinite spectrum. Usually we are tuned to our favorite frequency — physical reality— but we sometimes hear bleed-through from other stations. Some of us can tune to a wider range of frequencies, and some of us have the ability to listen to more than one station at a time.
>
> Perhaps with special training or with more openness, we could learn to broaden our individual spectrum. In principle, we are all capable of receiving all stations (Friedman, 1997, p. 206).

This suggests that there are arenas of communication going on all the time between living things that we are mostly unaware of. This is what Friedman refers to as the "hidden domain."

Paul Pearsall's, *The Heart's Code: Tapping the Wisdom and Power of Our Heart Energy* (1998), suggests that this is precisely what is going on. In this book, Pearsall explores the idea of cellular memory, especially in organ transplant operations. In many cases, the organ recipients begin to experience the memories of their organ donors. They may begin to have dreams about their organ donors and acquire the donor's dietary and behavioral patterns. The recipient's experience of their donor's life memories can be quite specific and accurate. In one case, a little girl, who had received the heart of another girl who had been murdered, began to have detailed memories of the murder; the murderer was later arrested and convicted based, in part, on her perceptions. In Claire Sylvia's, *A Change of Heart*, she outlines all of the physiological and psychological changes that accompanied her lung and heart transplant. She began to experience the dietary and lifestyle preferences of the 18-year male whose organs she received and who had died shortly before in a motorcycle accident. Although the medical advisors recommended she ignore these feelings, she felt compelled to explore them. Eventually she contacted the family of the donor so as to learn more about her new experiences and lifestyle changes. She found that her newfound perceptions and habits corresponded exactly to those of her organ donor. Thus, the donor's memories appeared to have been transplanted in addition to his organs.

These accounts demonstrate that thinking is an activity that is not limited to our brain: our organs and cells also think and possess memories, which they retain even outside of our bodies. They may also have methods of communication that defy conventional physical forms. While the exact method that allows such communication is unclear, it suggests that logical, rational thinking is only the tip of the iceberg when it comes to our body's innate intelligence.

Extraterrestrial Intelligence

Recent evidence points to the existence of extraterrestrials on and around Earth. People like Dr. Steven Greer, who runs the Center for the Study of Extraterrestrial Intelligence (www.Cseti.org), has provided us with credible eyewitness testimony from within the military and intelligence agencies (www.DisclosureProject.org). We are learning that extraterrestrial consciousness is tapped into the universal mind grid that permeates space-time. Thus, ETs are able to pilot their ships and communicate with one another using the etheric properties of their minds. In other words, they transmit and receive thoughts through telepathic means. This idea is attested by Ingo Swann whose viewing of extraterrestrial entities on the Moon was mentioned in an earlier chapter. Testimony by rocket scientist

David Adair, who has apparently seen large, non-Earthly space vehicles in secret facilities, supports that these ET artifacts are based on crystalline technologies that are semi-sentient; that is, they are aware of their pilots' thoughts. Aerospace technician Edgar Fouche's testimony also provides evidence that ET technology is crystalline based. This suggests a whole new level of technology based on entirely different principles than our fossil-fuel based mechanistic devices. If most ET civilizations were using our technology, we probably would have picked up their radio signals by now. However, it is more likely they use some sort of "etheric Internet" that works at the frequency of thought rather than in the realm of electromagnetics.

To meet the civilizations that design and use such machines, we must first become experts of our own awareness. This entails cultivating our inner resources and learning how to connect to the larger universe in a symbiotic and harmonious way. As I previously stated, before we meet the outer aliens, we need to meet the inner ones first. And of the two activities, the latter is the most important.

Accessing Subtle Energies—The Magic is Back

The previous discussion shows that our bodies can access and use etheric energies in automatic and spontaneous ways that are as yet unknown by science. These subtle energies are at this point well-documented and researched, while it is still unclear exactly what they are or how they specifically work. The main point is that these energies are built into our bodies and permanently available to all people. Resonant viewing and crop formations are just two of many ways to access these energies. Other well known methods include meditation, Tai Chi and Chi Kung, and various types of physical sports activities. The name of the game here is integration and coherency: any practice that furthers these objectives will serve that purpose. We don't need to wait for science to come up with an answer to explain these etheric principles. As these activities allow people to actively participate in the etheric, it is up to each individual to find their unique means for tapping into the unknown.

To advance our own personal and ecological integration, we do not need to learn anything new as much as we need to unlearn and forget anachronistic untruths about our personal limitations that we have been taught since childhood. Subtle energies are always present—it is the act of paying attention to them that activates their magic in our lives. We merely need to remember what we already know: that we are unlimited beings in a mysterious, infinite universe.

Postscript—A Moment in the Sun

IN THE SUMMER OF 2001, Midwest Research and the Institute for Resonance made three experimental formations in the area of Hilmarton, England. The farmer was paid for the use of his field and he was interested in what we were doing. The formations were made by six people using two to three "stomper boards" at a time. It took us about eight hours to do all three formations, some of which were done at night. All three circles showed changes in the electrostatic charges of the area of the formation. While we were not trying to prove that all formations are manmade, we were attempting to see if our formations could invoke the same "supernatural" forces often encountered in other formations. Although we did experience some equipment and battery failure just as we started to work on the formations, we did not encounter any balls of light or other extraordinary phenomena. Unfortunately, the farmer, not used to having that much public attention, cut the formations down soon after their construction, several weeks sooner than the harvest. We were able to ascertain from our experiment that humans can make large formations (our largest was about 300 feet across) with simple equipment like surveyor's tape and wooden boards. We found the experience quite challenging and recommend that other interested people try it themselves.

At the end of the first day we had made three formations. We made two small ones in the afternoon and then the larger one in the evening. We stopped working at about 11:00 p.m. Figure 47 shows what the field looked like the following morning and this is the picture that appeared on the Crop Circle Connector website (www.CropCircleConnector.com). We then proceeded to finish the larger formation that afternoon by flattening the crescent area. Figure 48 shows the large formation as it appeared when finished.

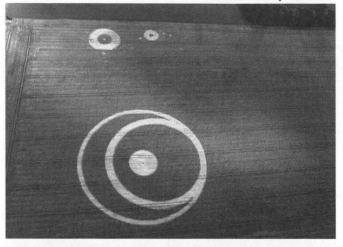

Figure 47: The Hilmarton Formations of 2001

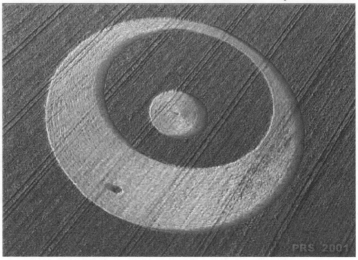

**Figure 48: The Main Hilmarton Formation
the Next Day After Completion**

To our surprise, a very similar formation (Figure 49) appeared within days at Gog Magog in the Cambridge area, a grueling three-hour drive from the Hilmarton area. We may never know who or what made this impressive formation, but it shows that crop circle phenomenon is intrinsically interactive and constantly evolving.

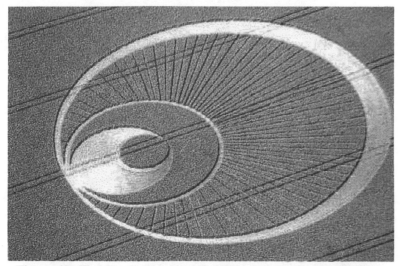

Figure 49: The Cambridge Angel, 2001   Photo © 2001 by Andrew King

In mid-September, the last English crop formation of the year 2001 appeared at Wabi farm (Figure 50). It was made by an acquaintance of mine and some of his circle-making comrades, with the permission of the farmer. The designer created the pattern according to aesthetic criteria and paid no special thought to any larger meaning. At a special Bashar channeling session held in Los Angeles on October 20, 2001, Bashar mentioned this formation and said it was a representation of the Sirius star system. This is interesting because the designer had no idea what he was making. It supports the ideas presented in this book: that crop formations represent a blending of energies from many different resonant sources. We do not need to analytically understand them for their magic to enter our lives.

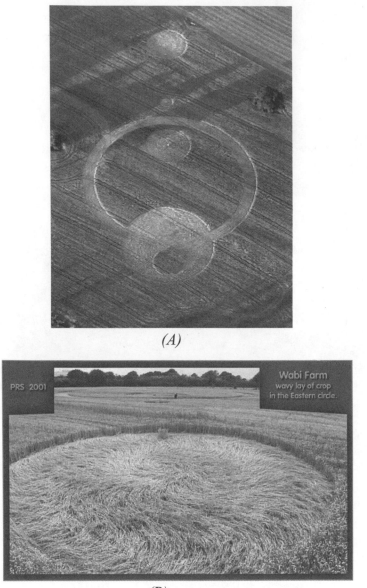

(A)

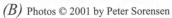

(B) Photos © 2001 by Peter Sorensen

Figures 50: Wabi Farm Formation, 2001

Bibliography

Abbot, Edwin. A. 1984. *Flatland: A Romance of Many Dimensions*. New York: New American Library.

Beniger, James. 1986. *The Control Revolution: the Technological and Economic Basis of the Information Society*. Cambridge, Massachusetts: Harvard University Press.

Bertman, Stephen. 1998. *Hyperculture: The Human Cost of Speed*. Westport, CT: Praeger.

Berry, Wendell. 1995. *Another Turn of the Crank*. Counterpoint: Washington, D. C.

Black, Edwin. 2001. *IBM and the Holocaust: The Strategic Alliance between Nazi Germany and America's Most Powerful Corporation*. New York: Crown Publishing.

Brown, Courtney. 1996. *Cosmic Voyage*. New York: Dutton.

Burke, James and Robert Ornstein. 1995. *The Axemaker's Gift: A Double-Edged History of Human Culture*. New York: Grosset/Putnam.

Chopra, M.D. Deepak. 1993. *Ageless Body, Timeless Mind: The Quantum Alternative to Growing Old*. New York: Harmony Books.

Collinge, William, Ph. D. 1998. *Subtle Energy: Awakening to the Unseen*. New York: Warner Books.

Corso, Philip J. 1997. *The Day After Roswell*. New York: Pocket Books.

Cottrell, Fred. 1972. *Technology, Man, and Progress*. ed. Ed Lemert. Columbus, OH: Charles E. Merril.

_____. 1955. *Energy and Society: The Relation Between Energy, Social Change, and Economic Development*. New York: McGraw-Hill Book Company.

Crichton, Michael. 1996. *The Lost World*. New York: Ballantine Books.

Dong, Paul and Thomas E. Rafill. 1997. *China's Super Psychics*. New York: Marlow and Company.

Durkheim, Emile. 1956. *The Division of Labor in Society*. New York: The Free Press.

Edwards, Betty. 1989. *Drawing on the Right Side of the Brain*. New York: Putnam.

Ellul, Jacques. 1964. *The Technological Society*. New York: Knopf.

Friedman, Norman. 1997. *The Hidden Domain: Home of the Quantum Wave Function, Nature's Creative Source*. Eugene, OR: The Woodbridge Group.

Gerber, Richard. 1988. *Vibrational Medicine: New Choices for Healing Ourselves*. Santa Fe: Bear and Company.

Gershon, Michael. D. 1998. *The Second Brain*. New York: Harper Perennial.

Giddens, Anthony. 1990. *The Consequences of Modernity*. Stanford, California: Stanford University Press.

Goldberger, Ary L., et al. 1990. "Chaos and Fractals in Human Physiology." *Scientific American*, February: 43-49.

Goldberger, Ary L. and Bruce J. West. 1987. "Fractals in Physiology and Medicine." *Yale Journal of Biological Medicine* 60: 41-35.

Goswami, Amit. 1993. *The Self-Aware Universe: How Consciousness Creates the Material World*. New York: G.P. Putnam's Sons.

Graff, Dale E. 1998. *Tracking the Wilderness: An Exploration of ESP, Remote Viewing, Precognitive Dreaming and Synchronicity*. Boston: Element Books.

Haselhoff, Eltjo H. 2001. *The Deepening Complexity of Crop Circles: Scientfic Research & Urban Legends*. Berkeley, CA: Frog, Ltd.

Hein, Simeon. 2000. "Electromagnetic Anomalies and Scale-Free Networks in British Crop Formations." *The Circular* 38: 35-8.

_____. 1995. "From Weber to Mandelbrot: Temporal Rationalization and the Fractal Flattening Effect." *Technological Forecasting and Social Change* 48(2): 189-210.

Holling, C. S. 1986. "The Resilience of Terrestrial Ecosystems: Local Surprise and Global Change." Pp. 292 - 316 in *Sustainable Development of the Biosphere*, edited by W. C. Clark and R. E. Munn. New Rochelle: Cambridge University Press.

Howe, Linda Moulton. 2000. *Mysterious Lights and Crop Circles*. New Orleans: Paper Chase Press.

Illich, Ivan. 1973. *Tools for Conviviality*. New York: Perennial Library.

Jackson, Wes. 1987. "The Information Implosion." *Altars of Unhewn Stone.* San Francisco: North Point.

Jaegers, Beverly. 1998. *The Psychic Paradigm: A Psychic Reveals the Secrets of Unlocking Your Own ESP Abilities.* New York: Berkeley Books.

Krapf, Phillip. 1998. *The Contact Has Begun: The True Story of a Journalist's Encounter with Alien Beings.* Carlsbad, CA: Hayhouse.

Lerner. Michael. 2000. *Spirit Matters.* Charlottesville, VA: Hampton Roads.

Macy, Mark H. 2001. *Miracles in the Storm: Talking to the Other Side with the New Technology of Spiritual of Contact.* New York: New American Library.

Maki, Masao. 1997. *In Search of Brazil's Quantum Surgeon: The Dr. Fritz Phenomenon.* San Francisco: Cadence Books.

Marrs, Jim. 2000. *Psi Spies.* Phoenix, AZ: Alien Zoo Press.

_____. 1997. *Alien Agenda. Investigating the Extraterrestrial Presence Among Us.* New York: Harper Collins.

McKibben, Bill. 1993. *The Age of Missing Information.* New York: Penguin Books.

Mindell, Arnold. 2000. *Quantum Mind: The Edge Between Physics and Psychology.* Portland, OR: Lao Tse Press.

Moore-Ede, Martin. 1993. *The Twenty-Four Hour Society.* New York: Addison-Wesley Publishing Company.

Morehouse, David. 1996. *Psychic Warrior: Inside the CIA's Stargate Program*. New York: St. Martin's Press.

Mumford, Lewis. 1972. *The Myth of the Machine: The Pentagon of Power*. New York: Harcourt Brace Jovanovich.

_____. 1967. *The Myth of the Machine: Technics and Human Development*. New York: Harcourt Brace Jovanovich.

Norretranders, Tor. 1998. *The User Illusion: Cutting Consciousness Down to Size*. New York: Penguin Group.

Ogburn, W. F. 1957. "Cultural Lag as Theory." *Sociology and Social Research* XLI (January):167-73.

Ornstein, Robert. 1997. *The Right Mind: Making Sense of the Hemispheres*. New York: Harcourt Brace and Co.

Pert, Candice B. *Molecules of Emotion: Why You Feel the Way You Feel*. New York: Simon and Schuster.

Pearsall, Paul. 1998. *The Heart's Code: Tapping the Wisdom and Power of Our Heart Energy*. New York: Broadway Books.

Raeburn, Paul. 1995. *The Last Harvest: The Genetic Gamble that Threatens to Destroy American Agriculture*. New York: Simon and Schuster.

Reed, Jonathan and Robert Raith. 2000. *Link: An Extraterrestrial Odyssey*. Seattle, WA: Spectrum Infinity Press.

Rifkin, Jeremy. 1987. *Time Wars: The Primary Conflict in History*. New York: Simon and Schuster, Inc.

Roszak, Theodore. 1986. *The Cult of Information: A Neo-Luddite Treatise on High-Tech, Artificial Intelligence, and the True Art of Thinking.* Berkeley: University of California Press.

Schnabel, Jim. 1997. *Remote Viewers: The Secret History of America's Psychic Spies.* New York: Dell Publishing.

Schachtman, Tom. 1995. *The Inarticulate Society: Eloquence and Culture in America.* New York: The Free Press.

Shiva, Vandana. 1997. *Bio Piracy: The Plunder of Nature and Knowledge.* Boston: South End Press.

Stoll, Clifford. 1999. *High Tech Heretic: Why Computers Don't Belong in the Classroom and Other Reflections by a Computer Contrarian.* New York: Doubleday.

_____. 1995. *Silicon Snake Oil: Second Thoughts on the Information Highway.* New York: Doubleday.

Swann, Ingo. 1998. *Penetration: The Question of Extraterrestrial and Human Telepathy.* Rapid City, South Dakota: Ingo Swann Books.

Sylvia, Claire. 1997. *A Change of Heart.* New York: Time Warner.

Talbott, Michael. 1992. *The Holographic Universe.* New York: Harper Perennial.

Targ, Russell and Jane Katra. 1999. *The Heart of the Mind: How to Experience God Without Belief.* Novato, CA: New World Library.

_____. 1998. *Miracles of Mind: Exploring Nonlocal Consciousness and Spiritual Healing,* Novato, CA: New World Library.

Toffler, Alvin. 1990. *Powershift: Knowledge, Wealth, and Violence at the Edge of the 21st Century*. New York: Bantam Books.

_____. 1971. *Future Shock*. New York: Bantam Books.

Van Creveld, Martin. 1989. *Technology and War: From 2000 B.C. to the Present*. New York: The Free Press.

Veblen, Thorstein. 1915. *Imperial Germany and the Industrial Revolution*. New York. Macmillan.

Weber, Max. 1978. *Economy and Society*, ed. Guenther Roth and Claus Wittich. Berkeley: University of California Press.

_____.1958. *The Protestant Ethic and the Spirit of Capitalism*. New York: Charles Scribner's Sons.

Weizenbaum, Joseph. 1976. *Computer Power and Human Reason: From Judgement to Calculation*. New York: W. H. Freeman.

Winner, Langdon. 1986. *The Whale and the Reactor: A Search for Limits in an Age of High Technology*. Chicago: The University of Chicago Press.

Young, Michael. 1988. *The Metronomic Society: Natural Rhythms and Human Timetables*. London: Thames and Hudson.

Zeleny, Milan. 1991. "Cognitive Equilibrium: A Knowledge-Based Theory of Fuzziness and Fuzzy Sets." *International Journal of General Systems* 19:359-381.

Index

Relevant Websites

www.Bashar.org
www.BioMindSuperPowers.com
www.CircleMakers.org
www.CropCircleConnector.com
www.CropCircleInfo.com
www.CropCircleResearch.com
www.CropCircles.org
www.CropCircleSpirit.com
www.CropCirclesRevealed.com
www.CrViewer.com
www.Cseti.org
www.DisclosureProject.org
www.ESPResearch.com
www.Farsight.org
www.GoRemoteViewing.com
http://Home.Clara.Net/LucyPringle
http://InvisibleCircle.de/uk
www.Ioon.net/CropCircles/index
www.Irva.org
www.Issseem.org
www.JimMarrs.com
www.LargerUniverse.com
www.PantaFueFuki.com
www.RvConference.org
www.Rviewer.com
www.TheNoiseRoom.com
www.TotalHumanSolution.co.uk
www.TruthSeekers.freeserve.co.uk
www.UFOCongress.com
http://UniversityOfLife.users2.50megs.com/
www.WorldITC.org

Www.MountBaldy.com
"Experience the Magic . . ."

About the Author

Simeon Hein received his Ph. D. in sociology from Washington State University in 1993. His dissertation focused on the role of technology in social and economic change, specifically how modern technology destroys information and interferes with natural evolutionary processes. He once taught social research methods and statistics at the university level. Now, he runs the Institute for Resonance (www.ResonantViewing.org) in Boulder, Colorado: a 501 (c)3 non-profit organization that specializes in instructing people in the art of resonant viewing and the scientific study of crop circles.

Dr. Hein first learned about viewing at the Farsight Institute in Atlanta in 1996 and has also studied with government-trained viewers. In conjunction with Midwest Research, he investigates the subtle-energy effects of crop circles and other related phenomena. He plays acoustic guitar and also writes and records his own music.

Www.MountBaldy.com

"Experience the Magic . . ."

Quick Order Form

Opening Minds: A Journey of Extraordinary Encounters, Crop Circles, and Resonance
by Simeon Hein, Ph.D.

 By mail: Send this form to **Mount Baldy Press**, P. O. Box 469, Boulder, CO 80306-0469
Email: Orders@mountbaldy.com

 By phone: **BookMasters** (Mansfield, OH), 1-800-247-6553, www.AtlasBooks.com

By secure server from the **Mount Baldy Store:** www.ExtraordinaryEncounters.com
Available as an eBook from www.1stBooks.com

Enclose cash, check, or credit card information for $19.95 per book (plus $1.49 tax for Colorado residents), and $5.00 (add $1.00 for each additional book) for Priority Mail shipping. International, add $10.00 per book (estimate) for air shipping (add $3.00 for each additional book).

Yes! I want ___ books. Please send them to the following address:

Name:_____

Address:_____
_____
_____

Email:_____
Credit Card_____
Exp.Date_____

Signature_____